Public Management as Art, Science, and Profession

Public Management as Art, Science, and Profession

Laurence E. Lynn, Jr.
The University of Chicago

Chatham House Publishers, Inc.
Chatham, New Jersey

PUBLIC MANAGEMENT AS ART, SCIENCE, AND PROFESSION

CHATHAM HOUSE PUBLISHERS, INC.
Post Office Box One
Chatham, New Jersey 07928

PUBLISHER: Edward Artinian
COVER DESIGN: Lawrence Ratzkin
PRODUCTION SUPERVISOR: David Morris
COMPOSITION: Bang, Motley, Olufsen
PRINTING AND BINDING: R.R. Donnelley & Sons Company

LIBRARY OF CONGRESS CATALOGING-IN-PUBLICATION DATA
Lynn, Laurence E., Jr. 1937–
      Public management as art, science, and profession
  / Laurence E. Lynn, Jr.
        p.   cm.
      Includes bibliographical references and index.
      ISBN 1-56643-034-8 (pbk.)
      1. Public administration—Study and teaching (Higher)—
United States. 2. Public administration—United States. 3. Policy
sciences—Study and teaching (Higher)—United States.   I. Title.
JF1338.A3U56   1996
350—dc20   95-41793
                                                      CIP

Manufactured in the United States of America
  10   9   8   7   6   5   4   3   2   1

CONTENTS

Contents

ACKNOWLEDGMENTS

Students, colleagues, friends, scholars, and public managers at all levels of government, whom I encountered at work, in classrooms, and in the literature, have contributed to my understanding of public management. I thank them all.

As editor of the *Journal of Policy Analysis and Management,* Lee Friedman saw what he regarded as an important agrument in what might otherwise have been merely a literature survey. His advice and encouragement were instrumental in the creation of this book.

Special thanks are due my wife Pat and my daughter Katie, who allowed me to use our home as my workshop.

Introduction

Public management has become an important domain of scholarship and teaching within two academic communities: public administration and public policy. The purpose of this book is to give definition to this domain. More specifically, it is about the relationship between knowledge and practice in public management and about the role of universities in creating and sustaining this relationship.

The justification for using "public management" as a focus for academic inquiry is, as yet, essentially arbitrary, and the term retains an irreducible ambiguity. Is public management a subfield of public administration, or is it the other way around? Is it an extension or an aspect of public policymaking or the other way around? Is it a concept with identifiable theoretical foundations, a logical extension of more basic inquiry, or is it a transitional subject and, as such, a progenitor of theory? Perhaps public management is no more than a label for the marketing of courses and training programs concerned with an administrative activity that is essentially an indeterminate practice.

That such questions have no widely accepted answers can be explained by the fact that "public management" did not originate as a term of scholarship: a way to define or clarify. Instead, it began as a term of art expressing a jurisdictional claim by "new" graduate programs in public policy to a domain "owned" until the early 1970s, when public policy programs began to proliferate, by another field:

so-called traditional public administration. As I argue later in this book, issues concerning jurisdiction are central to understanding the evolution of public management as a teaching and research enterprise. Despite the questionable legitimacy of its birth, the term has been appropriated by teachers and scholars in the academic community to provide a theme for their work, and so the intellectual questions must be taken seriously, at least within the academy.

In addressing such questions, I begin and end with the following argument. An identifiable group of actors in political life, called for convenience "public managers," collectively perform a significant part of the executive function in government. Public managers are the human capital of the government's executive capacity. The contributions of these actors are shaped and constrained by diverse authorities: constitutions, statutes, administrative arrangements and practices, court orders, and political custom. Some public managers are elected and may or may not be subject to term limits. Some are appointed by elected officers and serve either at their pleasure or for fixed terms. Some are selected according to the statutes and procedures of merit systems, and though such career managers may be reassigned and their jobs redefined, they cannot be removed except for cause.

An executive branch of government, whether at federal, state, or local level, is composed of officials who collectively share executive authority. Executive authority—the authority to direct the activities of others—is also shared by officials of other branches of government (i.e., legislatures and courts) and by a variety of regulatory bodies, independent authorities, and special districts with only attenuated ties to an elected administration. The intellectual domain of public management logically encompasses all officials and agencies sharing executive authority and their collective impact on public policy.

In practice, the intellectual domain of public management is partitioned. Elected executives are the province of a specialized community of scholars, largely within the discipline of political science, who focus primarily on the presidency and rarely on governors and mayors. Appointed executives have come to be the province primarily of scholars within graduate programs in public policy analysis and management.[1] Career executives and managers are the province primarily of scholars associated with programs in public administration.[2] Executives with specialized responsibilities or auspices, and the exercise of executive authority by other branches of government, are the preserves of scholars occupying niches in diverse fields of inquiry: law and economics, organization studies, administrative law, and the like.

This partitioning of the domain distorts the study of public management and, ultimately, our understanding of it. Scholars in the two largest academic provinces, public policy and public administration, have tended to be—there is no better word for it—provincial. Sociologically they fraternize or collaborate infrequently, and intellectually they cite one another's work irregularly.

The provincial boundary markers constitute various attitudes toward what has long been known as the politics-administration dichotomy, the notion that policymaking and its administration are governed by different principles and actors and require different kinds of specialized knowledge, training, and socialization. The descriptive accuracy of this dichotomy was discredited over half a century ago. It survives in a sociological and political sense because it justifies the jurisdictional claims of the two communities of public management scholars and teachers, as well as practitioners trained and socialized in one or the other of these communities who value the security or status of a circumscribed role.

The public policy community is on the politics side of the divide. Its territorial claims come in the guise of the "implementation perspective" on public policy and in the emphasis on "the politics of management" as practiced by political appointees. The goal is effective policy management on behalf of identifiable social outcomes legitimated—the emphasis varies—by substantive coherence, by voting constituencies and stakeholders, or by deliberative processes.

1. These programs constitute the academic institutional members of the Association for Public Policy Analysis and Management (APPAM).

2. Such programs are associated primarily with the National Association of Schools of Public Affairs and Administration (NASPAA). NASPAA and APPAM have a number of joint members.

The public administration community is on the administration side of the divide. Interest focuses on the roles and status of career civil servants and the organizations that employ them; there are constant references to civil servants' "political masters" on the policy side of the divide. The goal is competent administrative management and the creation and maintenance of effective organizations legitimated by constitutional and statutory authority.

Because it lacks intellectual or empirical substance, the dichotomy creates a porous boundary that is easily, although not frequently enough, crossed. But the situation appears to be in flux. Indeed, as I discuss in chapter 6, considerations of mission and method appear to be pulling the two provinces even farther apart. To overcome these tendencies, a relatively small interprovince group of scholars and teachers has since 1991 conducted a series of biannual National Public Management Research Conferences. Participants in these conferences view the provincial boundary as getting in the way of useful intellectual exchange. This book views it as promoting the growth of a cross-border community of mutual interest in public management, perhaps to the point where community members, like the Kurds of Turkey and Iraq, can assert a claim of jurisdiction over their artificially bifurcated territory.

Is it a territory of much intrinsic interest? Or is it a rhetorical device for instilling a useful thematic unity into professional training but barren of scholarly significance? Public managers are presumptively influential in shaping the policies and performance of the state. But how influential? Are they more than epiphenomenal? Are their contributions important enough to notice or to study? The premise of this book is that public managers are influential enough, in theory and in practice, to justify public management as an organizing topic for scholarship and teaching. The extent of this influence is controversial, however, and scholars and teachers in many cognate fields doubt that this influence amounts to much. Hence confirmation of influence is needed to justify attracting resources to the topic of public management.

There is, of course, the appearance of influence—individuals in visible positions of authority having an apparent impact on public policy and governmental performance—and the supportive testimony of practicing incumbents who believe they can change the course of events. But appearances can be deceptive and supportive testimony can be self-serving or deluded. If public management is to be a scholarly field, self-serving claims must be examined critically. The task of scholarship is to penetrate appearances to discover underlying truth.

This book constitutes an effort to focus the search for an underlying truth. While it draws on and extends my previous work on this topic, the argument is more directly an outgrowth of an ongoing debate among scholars and teachers in the previously identified communities of public policy and public administration. The argument is over the meaning of a term—public management—that, though in widespread use, is more of a "hook" for certain kinds of teaching and research than a coherent conceptual construct, useful because it has verisimilitude rather than for having an agreed-upon intellectual content.

Interestingly enough, the debate so far has produced little more than impressionistic knowledge concerning public managers' actual impact on events. Do public managers, as individuals in their own right and holding other influential factors constant, create legacies of significant success or failure—are they significant independent variables in a theory of policy outcomes or organizational effectiveness? What are their characteristic contributions? Should we care who they are (i.e., about the political appointment process and biographical details) or how skillfully they perform their duties? Or do public managers leave only faint footprints—do they at best only mediate the influence of larger political, structural, economic, or social forces? That the field's answer favors significant influence is primarily an article of faith based on practice wisdom and casual observation, not an empirically demonstrated truth.

The debate has instead featured arguments concerning the subject's epistemology. Is the subject's knowledge base shrewdly observed experience distilled into authoritative prescriptions (or "best practice"), or is it insights based on applications of theory or heuristic models distilled into contingent propositions (or rules) concerning the effectiveness of managerial actions? A popular duality casts public management as either "craft/art" (in an Aristotelian sense) or "science" (in a Platonic sense). The field's purpose is alternately viewed as providing either positive knowledge or normative guidance for practice.

Issues concerning the authority or jurisdiction of the field of public management, though implicit in the views of the communities' scholars, are only occasionally alluded to in debates over content and epistemology. Defining a domain of specialized knowledge, whether a craft or a science, constitutes a claim of jurisdiction for its producers and practitioners. Some definitions imply that public management is a profession subject to externally validated qualifications and standards. Other definitions imply less: successful practice is workmanlike but not much more.

This issue has important implications for the university's role in training practitioners. Thus I address the question of the sense in which public management is not only an art or a science but a profession, that is, a domain with a valid claim to possessing the specialized knowledge that justifies a credentialing, legitimizing function by universities.

The reason for introducing jurisdictional considerations into the debate is that arguments over the intellectual content of public management frequently obscure not only the jurisdictional implications of the conclusions reached but also the fact that positions on epistemological questions are taken *because* of their jurisdictional implications. As I noted earlier, the term originated in a jurisdictional claim. Moreover, to argue, as I and others have done, that knowledge for practice is more usefully derived from theory-based heuristic models than from uncritically received practitioner self-reports has important jurisdictional implications.

Acceptance of the former argument tends to lower entry barriers to those individuals, schools, and programs able and willing to apply formal reasoning (e.g., rational choice models) to actual management problems. But it raises barriers for those programs lacking the necessary technical proficiency or disciplinary identification. Field building through ethnographic methods, in contrast, privileges individuals and programs with close ties to practitioners and "hands-on" approaches and relegates to irrelevance the more academic approaches.

Introduction

The argument in this book is that the field of public management, conceived of as the executive function in government, will have a stronger, more enduring, and more useful identity as a domain of scholarship and of professional activity if its contributors and practitioners (1) establish intellectual foundations in those scholarly fields and subfields that can illuminate the executive role in government; (2) develop habits of reasoning, intellectual exchange, and criticism appropriate to a scholarly field; and (3) apply their intellectual skills in a distinctively useful way to answering the central question of public management. That question must be, Under what circumstances, and how, do executives and the executive function make a difference to the success of public policy and public agencies? As a field of teaching and research, public management should balance art and science toward achieving social utility and professional respect. This argument is developed in six chapters.

In chapter 1 I establish as ground for the intellectual development of public management the political dynamics by which the executive function in the American state has evolved from its federalist origins to the present and by which it will continue to evolve. I raise the question as to the relative importance of foreground actors and background institutions in an accurate depiction of the American state.

The next two chapters appraise public management from the perspectives of each of its two provinces. Chapter 2 surveys the work of scholars in the public administration community whose goal is knowledge for understanding the executive function construed as administrative management, that is, as contributing to effective organizational performance within a constitutional framework. In chapter 3 I survey how public management scholars in the public policy community have sought to create foundation knowledge for understanding the executive function in government construed as policy management, that is, as achieving the diverse, ambiguous, conflicting goals of public policy.

The following two chapters offer a potentially unifying view —but not a compromise view—of the subject of public management. In chapter 4 I draw contrasts between experiential and analytical perspectives on public management and argue for the propriety of emphasizing the analytic dimension of managerial performance. Chapter 5 sketches the knowledge base appropriate to "analytical practice," outlining concepts and tools that can serve as foundations for scholarship and teaching for practice thus conceived.

The jurisdictional implications of various ways to create and apply knowledge to professional practice are explored in chapter 6. I show how claims to intellectual authority are differentially sustained by those who view the foundations of knowledge as essentially experiential and by those who see the foundations of knowledge as essentially analytical. I argue that in order to flourish in the academy, to achieve credibility as a profession, and ultimately to enhance the scholars' contributions to effective practice, an analytic approach is essential.

Public executives, whose practice public management scholars and teachers aspire to inform, are designing the institutions and agencies of health-care finance and delivery. They are attempting to manage public welfare agencies toward results that will sustain Americans' commitment to social justice. They are attempting to govern partially decentralized school systems and community-based systems of mental health care in order to maintain and enhance the value of America's human capital. Public executives are the key actors in reinventing, reengineering, rethinking, and retooling regulation, the federal system, and the application of science to human betterment. Establishing intellectual foundations for advising them in this work, vital for our democracy and for the credibility of democratic institutions, is the domain of public management scholarship and teaching.

1

FIGURE AND GROUND:
PUBLIC MANAGEMENT AND POLITICS

Energy in the Executive is a leading character in the definition of
good government.

— Alexander Hamilton

P ublic rancor toward government is an enduring and ironic
feature of American democracy. Especially in recent years,
acute dissatisfaction with government—more specifically,
with politicians and the bureaucracy—has become a leitmotif of
public discourse and, a fortiori, of governmental administration. Citizens seem to take it for granted that, despite the best efforts of managers, "government doesn't work."

Domesticated Government

Unique among the world's democracies, American government is accountable to the freely expressed will of the people; popular sover-
eignty is more than myth, elections more than ceremony. Americans
have shown that they will countenance, by international standards
(Riggs 1994), no more than a relatively weak executive and a malle-
able, risk-averse bureaucracy. Yet Americans are prone to regard the
government they have sanctioned, however domesticated it may
seem from a world view, as beyond their control or even their com-

prehension, imposed on them by unelected "others" rather than chosen by the people.

Popular contempt for government and its officers often occurs in understandable reaction to corruption, favoritism, and incompetence. Impatience with the dilatory nature of legislative and bureaucratic politics, or, alternatively, with hasty, ill-conceived acts, also fuels criticism. Reprisals against offending incumbents and parties at election time are logical expressions of these kinds of dissatisfaction.

Public discontent need not have a specific justification. Regimes of ordinary competence are also condemned and replaced simply because they become emblematic of bureaucracy or of a tiresome status quo: a convenient scapegoat for frustrated voters. Though seemingly promiscuous, this practice of change for its own sake is also to be expected. If citizens insist, as Americans do, that they are sovereign, and if they differ among themselves as to what the public good requires, then candidates for office will compete vigorously to win control over the powers of the state to tax, spend, and regulate property rights. The resulting uncertainty of administration is an inevitable concomitant of our political practices and, it can be argued, the price we pay for long-term regime stability.

But the tone can get nasty, the instability counterproductive, the pressures on public officials debilitating. If voters and resources are to be mobilized to support a change of control from insiders to outsiders—from entrenched interests to "the people," from liberals to conservatives, or vice versa—denunciations of the status quo must be convincing. The electorate is congenitally suspicious of entrenched bureaucratic power and inclined to regard public management as an oxymoron; they will believe the worst. As a consequence, rarely do electoral contests turn on the substance of policies and the demonstrated competence of particular officials; seldom do they feature evidence and rational argument, at which voters' eyes might glaze over. Electoral agendas are more likely to be largely symbolic and feature ideological poses and contrived charges of mismanagement designed to embarrass incumbents and manipulate voters to anger. Whether particular officials and policies are in fact guilty of negligence or any of the many "——feasances" is beside the point; they must be made to seem so.

Owing to the dynamics of social and economic change mediated by political ambition, the administration of the American state has been periodically heated by fevers not just of change but of reform, that is, the redesign of governmental institutions and practices. In consequence, public managers have been the experimental white mice of American politics, forced to seek routes to accountability through shifting and ever more elaborate mazes of constraint. Administrators of public policies face pressures that test and often defeat even the most skilled among them while seeming to reward reactive and self-seeking opportunists.

An inevitable result is ineffectual public management. Vigorous and far-seeing administration is hardly ever the result of reform, at least not for long, for the shadow of future reprisals for bungling hangs ominously over the present. Widespread public cynicism among citizens—most do not even bother to vote anymore—promotes equally widespread aversion to taking risks that might jeopardize the careers of those called on to execute public mandates.

Contested Authority

The perils of executive governance are not a product of the television age or Watergate or other recent blows to civic faith. Nor are they traceable to the advent of the modern administrative state, which is usually thought to have occurred following the Civil War and to have been inaugurated with the creation, beginning in the 1880s, of a professional, tenured civil service (Rosenbloom 1994; Skowronek 1982). The story of the political dynamics that are the ground of public management begins with the debates among authors of *The Federalist* concerning the nature of executive power in a constitutional republic in which executive authority is ambiguous by design (Mansfield 1989).

The Premodern Era

The definition of the president's role as an administrator of government began with the first Congress, more or less in conformity with the ideas of Alexander Hamilton favoring a strong executive.

Though administrative responsibility would surely be delegated to subordinate officials, Hamilton in *The Federalist* No. 72 insisted that

> the persons ... to whose immediate management these different matters are committed, ought to be considered as the assistants or deputies of the chief magistrate, and on this account, they ought to derive their offices from his appointment, at least from his nomination, and ought to be subject to his superintendence.

Federalist administrations established Hamilton's model of executive authority. Early Congresses gave the president a continuing grant of administrative power to prescribe the duties of the heads of departments and their obligations to act in accordance with his instruction (White 1948). The crucial test of the extent of that authority was over whether the president could remove an officer without the consent of Congress, an authority he was granted by Congress in its first session in 1789. Although George Washington chose not to interfere in the conduct of departmental business, early practice confirmed the unity of the chief executive and the subordinate role of departmental officials, whom Washington would regularly convene as a group known as the president's cabinet.

The advent of Jacksonian democracy and the rise of populist political parties in the first half of the nineteenth century were soon to influence executive practice in government as profoundly as had Hamilton's views on the preeminence of executive authority. The heads of federal departments were uniquely exposed to the separate and often conflicting demands of what Leonard D. White (1954, 87) termed "statecraft, politics, and administration." With the emergence of the party system, cabinet appointments became distinctly political, and cabinet officers spent a great deal of time in partisan political activity.[1] Though the notion of objective qualifications for

1. Of the seventy-six cabinet officers who served between 1829 and 1861, the great majority were former congressmen and more than half held office less than two years (White 1954, 88).

public service began to be introduced, the democratic spirit of the time held that the "common man," qualified by virtue of loyal political service and ties to elected officials, ought to be the mainstay of government officialdom, an idea corrupted into the adage "To the victor belong the spoils."

In the decades following the Civil War, the scope and magnitude of executive branch responsibilities grew and the trappings of the modern state—bureaus, programs, regulations—started to appear. In reaction, Congress began to play an even more assertive role in shaping the evolution of public administration. Existing executive departments were authorized by Congress to expand and new offices were created, but Congress also began to create numerous independent boards and commissions to exercise powers "which Congress did not deem it advisable to intrust to a department, bureau, or even to an independent service under the direction of a single officer" (Short 1923, 440).

Further, Congress initiated numerous inquiries into bureau and departmental operations in the name of responsiveness and efficiency. Executive branch officials of the period spent an inordinate amount of time responding to these inquiries. Woodrow Wilson wrote in 1885: "... unquestionably, the predominant and controlling force, the centre and source of all motive and all regulative power, is Congress" (quoted in White 1958, 47).

Congress did not display great ability in its managerial role. Congressional and party dominance of the executive threatened the integrity and competence of governmental administration to the point that the pendulum started to swing back toward the enhancement of executive authority. As the state gradually assumed greater responsibilities in ensuing decades, nonprofessional administration of public functions proved increasingly unsatisfactory to an urbanizing, business-oriented middle class. Reformers argued that a competitive civil service would increase the efficiency and the moral authority of government. The blatant corruption of the administration of President Ulysses S. Grant and the assassination of President James A. Garfield in 1881 by a disgruntled office seeker built irresistible momentum for reform. The Civil Service Reform League was formed in 1881, and by 1883 patronage was viewed as an anachronism.

A Professional Government

Congress, heretofore reluctant to give up the influence it could exercise through patronage, bowed to the pressure and in 1883 passed the Civil Service (Pendleton) Act, which formally established a civil service system.[2] Relatively few officials were covered by the act's provisions at the outset, and it was not until 1920 that merit system employees secured tenure in office. But each successive administration brought in additional groups of government workers, thus sustaining what became an irreversible process of professionalization of the public service.

Along with the creation of the civil service system came an awakening concern with the size, expense, coordination, and overall efficiency of government. From the 1880s to the 1920s, the growing power of large organizations—corporations, unions, urban political machines—threatened to overwhelm private and public institutions and values. Whether classified as Mugwumps, populists, or progressives, Americans turned to the federal government to protect the integrity of the individual, the small businessman, and private property in general. Of this Progressive era, R.E. George wrote in 1916:

> So long as the government business was a small scale industry, so long as it did not cost the taxpayer large sums of money to operate, so long as it did not come in close touch with the average citizen, it did not attract attention.... But the change in the size of the government's activities has set in motion forces which are rudely shocking the indifferent citizen.... In place of popular carelessness, is coming an intense public demand for efficiency. And the same influence is changing the old methods of operation through the introduction of experts and through the reorganization of government to secure greater responsibility. (George 1916)

The contemporary ring of this analysis cannot be missed.

2. Appointments to office based in part on merit demonstrated in competitive examinations had been employed as early as 1871 by Secretary of the Interior Carl Schurz, one of the relatively few cabinet officers of the era who could be regarded as a distinguished administrator.

Figure and Ground: Public Management and Politics

The first executive expression of sustained interest in administrative reform can be found in the actions of President Theodore Roosevelt. In pursuit of scientific, efficient, neutrally competent administration, Roosevelt created the Commission on Departmental Methods, headed by Assistant Secretary of the Treasury Charles Hallam Keep. Termed "a landmark of executive introspection" (Emmerich 1971, 39), the Keep Commission from 1905 to 1909 stimulated management improvements throughout government in such fields as accounting, records administration, personnel administration, and procurement.

Another landmark development was the Commission on Economy and Efficiency created by President William Howard Taft. Between 1910 and 1913, this commission, which included leading administrative reformers and political scientists such as its chairman, Frederick A. Cleveland, a director of the New York Bureau of Municipal Research, Frank Goodnow of Columbia University, and W.F. Willoughby, studied the administrative organization of the national government and a number of its agencies. Though of little practical impact, efforts such as this one produced a sophisticated understanding of the governmental process. In 1913, J.Y. Brinton wrote, in a tone that is, again, remarkably contemporary:

> Each succeeding Congress witnesses some new and significant responsibility imposed upon the administrative system, and touching more or less intimately a large portion of the people. The vexing problems of the future will no longer be the great constitutional problems of deciding what may be done, or even the broader political problems of deciding what should be done, but will be the purely administrative problems of establishing really effective ways and means of carrying out the public's will. (Brinton 1913)

The most important administrative reform movement of this era, the executive budget movement, was nourished by three distinct groups: reformers interested in promoting better planning to cope with mounting social problems; public administrators interested in administrative reorganization and improved management; and leaders in Congress, business, and government interested in executive control of public spending (Schick 1971). It culminated in the Budget and Accounting Act passed by Congress in 1921, which authorized creation of the Bureau of the Budget, headed by a presidential appointee not subject to Senate confirmation.

The primary result of the Budget and Accounting Act was to equip the president to become for the first time the administrative head of government as well as its chief political officer. President Warren G. Harding's first appointee to the post of budget director, General Charles G. Dawes, actively promoted executive control of the budget; and he set in place the momentum that would produce a steady expansion of the senior executive's role in federal resource allocation. Departmental officials, who from President Jackson's time had been, in effect, agents of Congress, were being drawn back toward the president's political and administrative sphere of influence.

In passing the Budget and Accounting Act of 1921, however, Congress simultaneously created the General Accounting Office (GAO) to assist Congress in exercising oversight of the administration of federal funds. During the same period, moreover, both the House and the Senate streamlined their appropriations procedures. Authority for appropriations bills was exclusively assigned to appropriations committees, which were enlarged and divided into specialized subcommittees. Congress was not about to be left impotent in the face of executive aggrandizement.

The depression and subsequent second world war of the century brought on further irreversible growth of executive government: a welfare state, a national security state, and a financial and commercial state. President Franklin Roosevelt and his advisers sought with only modest success to consolidate executive control over what Rosenbloom (1994) has called "a 'headless fourth branch' of government," the permanent bureaucracy. The President's Committee on Administrative Management (the Brownlow Committee) recommended measures to secure the administrative independence of the executive branch. The one change of enduring significance was the creation of the Executive Office of the President.

Yet at the same time, the New Deal was also strengthening the access of organized interests to government bureaus, and the idea of

"representative bureaucracy" became important in public administration (Rosenbloom 1994). Secretary of Labor Frances Perkins went
so far as to assert that public participation in New Deal programs
"is the modern substitute for the old town meeting and the old talk
around the stove" (Rohr 1986, 167).

Of course, Congress would react to the long buildup of executive branch powers during the Roosevelt years. Concern mounted
that Congress was no longer a coequal branch and that it had been
reduced to merely saying yes or no to executive proposals. (Roosevelt had made it a regular practice to submit his own detailed drafts
of legislation for congressional consideration.) In 1945, the House
and Senate created a Joint Committee on the Organization of Congress. The resulting Legislative Reorganization Act of 1946 authorized increased professional and clerical staff for standing committees
and made the Legislative Reference Service (now the Congressional
Research Service) a separate department of the Library of Congress.
Section 136 authorized and directed standing committees to exercise
continuous oversight of executive agencies and programs.

Political Administration

With the growth of federal programs and of the intergovernmental
grant system in the postwar years, Congress faced increased pressures to exercise oversight, compounded by their determination to
impose more checks on the power of the executive in reaction to
President Lyndon Johnson's dominance. The Legislative Reorganization Act of 1970 authorized increased staffing for committees and
funds for outside experts. It also increased the resources and program evaluation authority of the GAO. Congress began requiring
more evaluations and reports, instituting legislative vetoes, controlling impoundments, analyzing programs, and requiring periodic re-
authorizations of programs.

From the congressional perspective, the nearly thirty years between the passage of the Legislative Reorganization Act of 1946 and
congressional approval of the Budget Reform and Impoundment
Control Act of 1974 involved a frustrating and unequal struggle
with the executive branch over the "power of the purse." Many leg-

islators were alarmed at their own irresponsible tendencies to authorize high levels of spending or to use subterfuges such as "tax expenditures" and "backdoor financing" and then hold the president accountable for fiscal responsibility.

Political executives saw the same struggle from a somewhat different perspective. "Until 1975," said Elliot Richardson (1976, 58), "the process of Congressional choice was impulsive, random, and fragmented." Federal executives could expect to be drawn into and even become preoccupied with the trench warfare between congressional committees and the executive branch, to have their daily schedules hostage to the congressional "compulsion to legislate" (Richardson 1976, 58). They were often caught in the middle between the committees, on the one hand, and the Office of Management and Budget and the White House on the other. Richardson notes that "the imbalance from which the Congress suffers most is a matter not of power but of capacity for coherent action—the ability to weigh competing claims, formulate a consistent strategy, and arrive at a sound consensus" (Richardson 1976, 62).

Because Congress lacked the capacity for coherence, the executive branch also lacked it. No amount of coherence at the top of government organizations can withstand the undertow of congressional fragmentation expressed through authorization and appropriations processes. As Stephen Hess put it (1976, 145): "The power to legislate, especially to write the fine print, often [is] the power to determine the contours of administration."

The Budget Reform and Impoundment Control Act of 1974 was intended to restore the balance in favor of Congress. This act created the budget committees of both houses as well as the Congressional Budget Office (CBO). Around this central tension has sprung up competition among the CBO, the GAO, the Congressional Research Service (CRS) of the Library of Congress, and the Joint Economic Committee, and between these offices and the mushrooming number of "think tanks" and advocacy organizations, to "inform" the deliberations of public officials.

This constitutional struggle between the executive and legislative branches generated, as eddies and cross-currents from the main flow of events, a series of more specifically focussed administrative reforms.[3] From the Hoover commissions through the PPBS/ MBO/ZBB era to the Reagan administration's Grace Commission and the Clinton administration's National Performance Review, a series of attempts has sought to accommodate the interests of stakeholders in responsive, efficient, and effective government.

Each has left legacies: reorganization as a tool of leadership, incorporation of policy analysis into public policymaking, recognition of the budget as a policy document, and emphasis on program evaluation. Among the most important of these legacies to the field of public management is the emergence of the graduate programs in public policy that form the core membership of the Association for Public Policy Analysis and Management. Founded on the premise that modern policy management requires specialized training, these schools constituted the milieu within which the notion of an executive function in government, distinctive and worthy of serious study and preparation, took root and grew.

In general, however, the significance of particular reforms lies less in how each was conceived and executed than in what they reveal about the characteristic dynamics of public administration. In America, as in few other industrial democracies, public administration is about politics, and politics is about citizen control of the state.

Process or Result?

American government is inevitably Madisonian: driven toward a balancing of interests. Discernible in this story of continuing, even compulsive, reform, however, is an enduring tension between two American stereotypes that are emblematic of a duality in the American character. One stereotype, usually termed "Jeffersonian," idealizes democratic participation and deliberation. The other stereotype, usually termed "Hamiltonian," idealizes decisive action by purposeful and empowered executives. Versions of these stereotypes are in-

3. For a lively account of these reforms, see Downs and Larkey (1986).

voked by critics and reformers to build support for their proposals.

The Jeffersonian stereotype celebrates the town meeting in which citizens have influence in proportion to the extent and quality of their participation in public deliberation. The New England township was cited by Tocqueville as essential to liberty and the ability to resist despotic tendencies. Ideally, the distinction between state and society is intentionally indistinct, and the necessity of a professional bureaucratic class is both questioned and resented (Skowronek 1982). In contemporary manifestations—the ennobling of community and neighborhood, and faith in grassroots activism, as bulwarks against the distant, bureaucratic state—this stereotype fosters inclusiveness and responsiveness through the dispersal of authority, multidirectional accountability, an empowered public, collaborations between government and private sectors, and the primacy of democratic process over imposed blueprints or goals.

The Hamiltonian stereotype evokes the entrepreneur purposefully leading an effective organization and has inspired generations of advocates for a businesslike approach to government. Tocqueville (1969) quotes Hamilton on "the mischiefs of that inconstancy and mutability in the laws, which *form the greatest blemish in the character and genius of our governments.*" "The administration of government," wrote Hamilton (*The Federalist* No. 68, 444), "... falls peculiarly within the province of the executive branch." Moreover, to Hamilton, "the true test of a good government is its aptitude and tendency to produce a good administration."

This stereotype idealizes the stability of strong executive leadership, the efficiency of the assembly line, and the entrepreneurial spirit of the corporation that increases its earnings and market share through successful product development, technological innovation, and a productive and well-deployed workforce. It fosters tough-mindedness, efficient use of scarce resources, a commitment to shareholders, a necessary concentration of executive authority, and the primacy of "good administration" over process.

The tension between these stereotypes and the centrifugal forces that such tension creates surrounding public management are distracting to public managers. In the 1990s, in a spirit of compromise, hybrid stereotypes attempt to meld technological innovation and an entrepreneurial disposition toward risk taking—Hamiltonian concepts—with worker autonomy and devolution of control—Jeffersonian concepts—to create new forms of organization that are at once efficient in using scarce resources and effective in responding to the needs and claims of lower employees, clients, and citizens. Such forms aim to achieve measurable results, without the mediating distortions of hierarchy, through "civic discovery," quality circles, or other participative processes. The intellectual incoherence of these hybrids notwithstanding,[4] these new paradigms represent bids to transcend and disable the core tension of American democracy.

But this tension between process and result, form and substance remains unresolved because of those unique aspects of American history termed *American exceptionalism.* Democratic institutions were firmly established in America well before the concentration of economic power in a corporate business sector and other forces of modernization gave rise to the investing of regulatory and ameliorative power in government (Skowronek 1982). In completing the transition from the nineteenth to the twentieth century, an essentially "stateless" society was transformed into a more orderly one featuring permanent bureaucratic organizations staffed by specialists (Skowronek 1982).

Though bureaucracy's reach has from the outset been firmly constrained by constitutionally mandated separation of powers, Americans, inured to democracy before they were confronted with the need for strong government, are easily agitated by the image of a Leviathan state threatening liberty and the security of property. Ensuring that bureaucracy is effectively controlled by citizens and their representatives seems in the popular mind, nostalgic for "statelessness," to require eternal vigilance, and those who would represent them are always opportunistically prepared to agree.

There is, however, sharp disagreement over why vigilance is

---

4. A paradox associated with the work of Harvey Sapolsky (1967) holds that an innovative organization requires, at the same time, central authority that is too weak to interfere with spontaneous creativity yet strong enough to embrace and see to the implementation of creative ideas.

necessary. Liberals would use the mechanisms of democratic oversight and control to ensure that the positive goals of government are achieved and that "the public interest" is never lacking advocates or access. Conservatives would use the same mechanisms to ensure that the growth and reach of government are sharply constrained and that "private interests" can always keep an eye on things. But, as Paul Light (1995) has shown, both attempts come to the same thing: an aggrandizement of the executive authority of government, an extension of political property rights in the form of officials statutorily empowered to do what stakeholders want done, and an exacerbation of tensions between executives and citizens.

The politics of bureaucratic control are hardly this straightforward. In times of ascendancy or crisis, liberal and conservative parties both might advocate the strengthening of the executive, in effect delegating control of the bureaucracy to appointed officials if such delegations would strengthen party control over public policy. In times of virulent popular discontent with politicians, both liberals and conservatives might advocate antistatist reforms and accountability to the people. At any time, interest-oriented "middle-game" politics may lead to the deliberate creation of entrenched bureaucracies as a way of awarding political property rights to favored constituencies. In ordinary times, or absent veto- or filibuster-proof majorities, however, legislators of all persuasions are likely to cooperate in advocating and promising voters legislative control of bureaucracy, and legislation will be studded with terms of the art of legislative control: "ban," "enforce," "limit," "prohibit," "require," "restrict," "sanction," and the like.

Interestingly enough, scholars disagree over the extent to which the control of bureaucracy is in fact a structural problem requiring solutions. In one view, the lack of democratic accountability on the part of unelected, tenured bureaucrats is too obvious to require argument (Gruber 1987). The evidence is widespread popular dissatisfaction with particular acts of government. In more sophisticated versions of this view, the inability of legislatures to provide unambiguous, measurable mandates to executive agencies, reflecting their inherent weakness in resolving conflicts, has the effect of displacing the functions of politics—deciding who gets what—onto bureaucrats, who function beyond the view of the public according to self-generated rules (Brodkin 1987–88).

Critics of this rather conventional view argue that few bureaucrats in any agency at any level of government fail to perceive what is expected of them by elected and political authorities (Noll and Weingast 1987). Knowledge of these expectations, transmitted via a variety of formal and informal public-choice mechanisms, shapes bureaucratic cultures and behavior in subtle but unmistakable and strikingly effective ways. If bureaucrats occasionally seem intransigent, it is only because legislators are confused, divided, or inarticulate. From this perspective, politics is about embedding political "property rights," that is, formal access to the processes of policymaking and execution, in the formal structures of government. The acts of bureaucracy can be construed as the expressions of a kind of structure-induced equilibrium.

Figure or Ground?

The issue of bureaucratic control has an important bearing on the study and practice of public management. In the increasingly acrimonious contest over the control of public policy, attention has been directed at the agents of elected executives: the corps of appointed officials who serve at their pleasure and who provide immediate oversight and direction to public bureaus. With the spotlight on them, these appointed officials necessarily seek to establish their influence over the ranks of tenured managers, supervisors, and workers. The effective establishment by such officials of a domain of influence over public bureaus has become, in essence, the subject of the emergent subfield of public management.

Lacking constitutional sanction or prescription, the exercise of appointed and delegated authority is, therefore, a resultant. From this perspective, public management is a derivative notion, synthesizing efforts to define and legitimate a sphere of authority and a repertoire of behaviors for a formally undefined and politically suspect collection of public actors.

This state of affairs constitutes a practical, an intellectual, and an aesthetic problem. The problem is analogous to composing a photograph in which the observer must place a foreground figure and its background in an aesthetically appropriate balance. What one "sees" is a matter of interpretation, distance from the object, and the capabilities of the recording apparatus.

The background of public management comprises the formal tensions between the branches of government, the informal tensions between the competing stereotypes of governance, and the forums where these tensions are played out: legislatures and bureaucracies. The figures are the officeholders who attempt to interpret and mediate these tensions in performing the executive function in government. A picture of public management will reveal foreground figures in appropriate relationship to their background. But judgments differ as to how to compose the resulting picture, whether in effect to blur the background so that figures stand out or to zoom back and view the larger background in sharp focus, in which case foreground figures may shrink to insignificance.

Confusion concerning the relationship of figure and ground has distorted the study of public management and channeled it in unproductive directions. As David Rosenbloom has observed, American administrative reformers from Woodrow Wilson's time to the present are prone to advocate a remaking of the political system to serve the needs of better management rather than to develop better management to serve the purposes of the political system (Rosenbloom 1993). Advocacy of "reinvention," paradigm replacement, "reengineering," or such new age measures as flattening hierarchies or worker control or civic deliberation is nothing more than symbolic posing unless it can be shown to be part of a coherent model of political economy and an intelligible political strategy for improving governmental performance.

2

THE PUBLIC MANAGER
AS ADMINISTRATOR

We do not wish to suggest that nothing has changed in the world,
or that we would not write a different book today; but we are grat-
ified that our book retains, after forty years, such a modern tone.
— Herbert A. Simon and Victor A. Thompson

Alexander Hamilton had a coherent theory of public administration,[1] and James Madison (inspired by Thomas Hobbes)
had referred to a "science of government" in *The Federalist*
37 (p. 229). Yet virtually no systematic thought or study concerning
public administration occurred until the first decades of the twentieth century (Short 1923, 24). This is not surprising. Government
was limited, subordinate, and party controlled during this era; the
social sciences were embryonic; and universities were only beginning
to define their role in research.

The forces shaping an urbanizing, modernizing America were to
provide the impetus for the emergence of a professional field concerned with public administration just as the growth of the corporate business sector was to provide the impetus for training and

1. The papers dealing with issues of administration and the exercise
of executive authority are Nos. 68 through 77.

study in business administration. For over a century, the intellectual boundary and interior contours of public administration have been shaped by various exogenous and endogenous forces. By now, the field has a boundary encompassing virtually all aspects of governmental administration and containing peaks and valleys of usable knowledge.

Rainey (1992, 147) lists topics on which public administration's scholars claim with increasing clarity and consensus a well-developed body of knowledge and expertise:

> The scope and role of government and theoretical rationales for and against government action; the characteristics of the administrative branch (including the types of agencies and alternative forms of administrative action); the relations between the bureaucracy and other governmental institutions and actors, and the values and processes of democratic governance; the public policy process and the role of the bureaucracy in it; public finance and the governmental budgeting process; administrative law; organization theory, especially as it pertains to public and quasi-public organizations; and a variety of specific managerial responsibilities, including management of personnel, finances, physical resources (for example, buildings), and computer and information systems.

In effect, whatever is of concern to public officials is of concern to the profession that claims jurisdiction over their training, competence, and status.

While this breadth is appropriate for a profession concerned with governmental administration, it greatly complicates the establishment of foundations and paradigms for intellectual activity. We should not be surprised to see, as we will, that teachers and scholars establish many domains within this terrain and describe the whole of it in different ways. Among the newer domains is that of public management.

Public Administration as Ground

The professionalizing reforms of the late 1800s and especially the creation of a formally qualified civil service stimulated the first modern literature of public administration. The seminal contribution is Woodrow Wilson's "The Study of Administration" (1887), in which he argued that

> the objective of administrative study is to rescue executive methods from the confusion and costliness of empirical experiment and set them upon foundations laid deep in stable principle. It is for this reason that we must regard civil service reform in its present stages as but a prelude to a fuller administrative reform.

The University of Pennsylvania and Columbia University began to offer courses in public administration as early as 1888. The University of Chicago appointed the nation's first professor of public administration in 1899, and in 1900 Frank Goodnow of Columbia published perhaps the first public administration textbook (Goodnow 1900).[2] Gradually, a number of colleges and universities added courses on government and public administration to their political science and general liberal arts curriculums (Stone and Stone 1975). In 1913 the Committee on Practical Training for the Public Service of the American Political Science Association endorsed formal training for government careers and advocated direct contact between universities and government.

The growth of professional education in public administration was slow because of weak demand by any level of government for trained administrators and professionals. In 1928 Luther Gulick noted that "the amateur is still largely in control, specialization arises only through accident, and direct training for the profession of public administration is largely unknown" (p. 52). Though the federal civil service system would ultimately constitute the primary market for schools of public administration, demand in the first decades of this century was low. Not until 1938, when federal departmental personnel offices were formed and a civil service examination for nontechnical administrative positions was introduced, did the federal

2. In 1893 Goodnow had published the two-volume *Comparative Administrative Law*, the first American treatise on public administration.

government became a significant market for administrative talent (Stone and Stone 1975; Eggers 1975).

The serious study of public administration, and the evolution of education for public administrators, was given impetus by developments at the municipal, not the federal, level of government (Graham 1941; Mosher 1975). The major cities, with their swelling immigrant populations, deplorable living conditions, and corrupt politics, became rallying points for progressive reformers. In 1894 the first national conference for reform of city government was held. In 1904 Lincoln Steffens's *The Shame of the Cities* stirred reformers to action. In an attempt at a constructive responsive, the New York Bureau of Municipal Research was formed in 1906 to study the administration of New York City in a systematic and scientific manner. Among the beliefs underlying their work was that "the purpose of administration is to serve the requirements of ... society with the utmost efficiency and economy" (Wallace 1941, 12).

The research and writing of Frederick W. Taylor and his followers was a principal source of ideas for the scientific reform of municipal administration. In his seminal 1911 book *The Principles of Scientific Management,* Taylor argued that the objective of the scientific manager is to discover the best (i.e., most efficient) way to accomplish a given task. Attempts to apply the objectives and methods of "Taylorism" were widespread in business and in municipal government, and scientific management societies flourished in America and abroad.[3] The Bureau of Municipal Research, assisted by this movement, extended its ideas to the public functions of personnel administration, accounting, and the organization and management of other specialized government functions.

In 1911 the bureau organized a Training School for Public Service which served as the model for a professional and practical, as opposed to an academic, approach to training for public administra-

---

3. Theodore Levitt (1976, 96) has observed, however, that "It was not until 1975 that a manual was written on how to use Taylor's 94-year-old methods to enhance productivity in government and service organizations—and then it was the Japanese who published it." The manual he referred to is Mundel (1975).

tion. The idea of using so-called laboratory methods in training for public administration, precursor of today's experiential approaches to teaching, first found expression (Gulick 1928, 54). (In 1916 Robert Brookings founded the Institute for Government Research to apply bureau approaches to federal problems.) Throughout the succeeding two decades, the spreading home-rule and city-manager movements would constitute the principal market for trained public administrators. Additional demands would come from the state-level reorganization movement that was transforming state governments dominated by autonomous boards and commissions into governments organized around single-headed, multimission departments.

Influenced by its ties with the emerging academic social sciences, by the tightening grip of behavioralism in social science research, and by continuing orientation to the functional and routine management tasks of municipal and state government, public administration fully embraced the borrowed methodology of scientific management, with its overriding emphasis on operational efficiency, and thereby cut itself loose from its intellectual roots in politics and administrative law. From its first enunciation by Wilson and Goodnow, scientific administration, which stressed the separation of administration from politics and efficiency as the goal of administration, became the dominant idea in public administration from roughly 1910 to 1940. Taft's Commission on Economy and Efficiency, which was a model for activities at all levels of government, propagated the notion of scientific management. By the mid-1920s, two textbooks, Leonard D. White's *Introduction to the Study of Public Administration* (1926) and W.F. Willoughby's *Principles of Public Administration* (1927), established the dominance of the idea that scientific principles should govern public administration.

The "quintessential scientific management statement in public administration" (Bozeman 1979, 33) was Luther Gulick and Lyndall Urwick's *Papers on the Science of Administration,* published in 1937. Gulick drew heavily on the work of Henri Fayol, a French industrialist then little known in America, who is credited with being perhaps the first to devise a theory of management. "What is the work of the chief executive? What does he do?" Gulick asked. "The answer," he said, following Fayol, "is POSDCORB" (Gulick 1937, 13), which referred to the seven principles of public administration: planning, organization, staffing, directing, coordinating, reporting, and budgeting.

By 1933, dozens of educational institutions were offering training programs for careers in government or courses in public administration (Eggers 1975). Their orientation and content tended to reflect the interests of the academic political scientists who were working on problems of state and local government, many imitating the approach of the Bureau of Municipal Research.

As the New Deal wore on, a gradual shift of orientation toward federal and programmatic interests occurred, especially in the new educational activities that began during this period. The new challenge, Rowland Eggers observes, "was the superimposition of broad administrative and managerial skills on civil servants with specialized education and experience—making city managers, for example, out of civil engineers, and making welfare administrators out of social case workers" (Eggers 1975, 65). Reflecting a growing sense of jurisdiction, political executives were often warned to stay out of the way of the real managers. Said Schuyler Wallace in 1941:

> The very complexities of the management of a large department should tend to compel the politically appointed heads to delegate the actual management of the department's routine to professional administrators, and to confine their own activities to the determination of the broad lines of departmental policy, the maintenance of legislative contacts and the task of interpreting their departments to the body politic— *functions more nearly within their comprehension and grasp.* (Wallace 1941)

But the reigning orthodoxy of scientific administration was already beginning to crumble: it failed to fit the emerging reality of the modern federal government with its regulatory, social welfare, and economic management responsibilities. The orthodox doctrine failed to offer any concept of a top management perspective to guide departmental administrators. Various authors began to resurrect the role of politics in executive administration and criticized the emptiness of the narrow doctrine of efficiency as an administrative goal.

As early as 1921, W.F. Willoughby had argued that the administrative branch is under Congress, not the president, and that the president should be regarded as Congress's agent in managing the government. "The Danger Today," warned Marshall Dimock in 1936, "is in going too far in the formal separation between politics and administration ..." (Dimock 1936, 3). Carl J. Friedrich summed up the case against the doctrinaire insistence that politics and administration are separate pursuits in 1940:

> Public policy, to put it flatly, is a continuous process, the formation of which is inseparable from its execution. Public policy is being formed as it is being executed, and it is likewise being executed as it is being formed.... In so far as particular individuals or groups are gaining or losing power or control in a given area, there is politics; in so far as officials act or propose action in the name of public interest, there is administration. (Friedrich 1940)

An ostensible admirer of Gulick, Schuyler C. Wallace in 1941 nevertheless criticized public administration's tendencies toward intense specialization and deduction from abstract generalization. Although increasing "the minutiae of knowledge," he wrote, specialists have neglected "the reciprocal interaction of the parts and the whole ... especially as regards the legislature and politics in the highest sense of the term." Broad generalizations with little reference to the social context divorced the science of administration from "the realities of the situation" (Wallace 1941).

Orthodox doctrine was finished off as the dominant school of thought in public administration after World War II in a series of articles and books by Herbert A. Simon, Robert A. Dahl, Paul H. Appleby, Norton E. Long, Dwight Waldo, and Fritz Morstein Marx. The goals and directions of government activity were recognized to be as much the product of decisions and actions taken at middle levels of the bureaucracy as they are the result of deliberation and determination by Congress. Legislators were recognized to be as much and often more concerned with how policy is executed (i.e., with administration) as with its goals.

As the old orthodoxy crumbled and the "political" character of administration was recognized, a new concern arose: the loss of democratic control of administration (Mosher 1968). This fear was voiced by James Burnham in his 1941 classic, *The Managerial Revolution.*

> "Laws" today in the United States, in fact most laws, are not being made any longer by Congress but by ... leading "executive agencies." ... Indeed, most of the important laws passed by Congress in recent years have been laws to give up some more of its sovereign powers to one or another agency largely outside of its control.... In the new form of society, sovereignty is located in administrative bureaus. (Burnham 1941, 147–48)

Bureaus proclaim the rules, make the laws, issue the decrees.[4]

Francis E. Rourke called attention to the paradox underlying this concern. "This fear of bureaucracy often co-exists with another attitude with which it is in sharp contradiction—the feeling ... that bureaucrats are timid, unimaginative, and reluctant to make decisions" (Rourke 1984).

The fear that technocrats and managers would subsume the principal functions of government was attenuated by the recognition that Congress was in cahoots with these technocrats. Observed C. Wright Mills in *The Power Elite* (1956, 258):

> Increasingly, the professional politician teams up with the administrator who heads an agency, a commission, or a department in order to exert power with him against other administrators and politicians, often in a cut-and-thrust manner. The traditional distinction between "legislation" as the making of policy and "administration" as its realization has broken down from both sides.

The fear shifted to one that democratic control was being lost to narrow alliances of self-interest among congressmen, bureaucrats,

---

4. Cf. Max Weber's observation, in an allusion to the views of Karl Marx, that "for the time being, the dictatorship of the official and not that of the worker is on the march." Quoted in H. Gerth and C. Wright Mills (1946, 40).

and representatives of special interests. This latter notion, which became popularized in the term iron triangle, has become a kind of new orthodoxy. Ernest S. Griffiths characterized these associations as far back as 1939 as follows:

> One cannot live in Washington for long without being conscious that it has whirlpools or centers of activity focusing on particular problems.... It is my opinion that ordinarily the relationship among these men—legislators, administrators, lobbyists, scholars—who are interested in a common problem is a much more real relationship than the relationship between congressmen generally or between administrators generally. (Griffiths 1939, 182)

It is a short distance from this vintage perspective to Hugh Heclo's more recent notion of "issue networks" (Heclo 1979), given more rigorous formulation and empirical identity in the work of Edward O. Laumann and David Knoke (Laumann and Knoke 1987).

An elaboration of the complex webs of organizations and actors that constitute the domain of governance might seem to render the individual public manager, in a term sociologists are apt to use, as *epiphenomenal.* Another research tradition within public administration, perhaps for practical rather than theoretical reasons, has shown far more interest in public executives as influential foreground actors.

Public Officials as Figures

The "tendency towards the development in the heads of departments of powers of supervision, direction, and control" (Goodnow 1905, 138) began attracting interest early in this century (Fairlin 1905; Hill 1916; Short 1923). In keeping with the research orientation of the times, these studies tended to be descriptive and concerned with the formal functions and powers of the executive as defined by the Constitution, federal statutes, and judicial opinions and showed slight interest in official behavior. By the 1930s, studies of federal executives had become more cognizant of their actual activities and conduct. Public administration doctrines of that time, however, still in the grip of the notion that politics was a corrupting influence on competent administrators, stressed the separability of politics and administration, and ideas about executive responsibility were still overly formal and abstract.

With the unprecedented administrative developments of the New Deal—the wholesale creation of new executive agencies to deal with social ills of every description—students of public administration were stimulated to undertake analyses of the actual experiences of government executives in the light of their steadily growing responsibilities, and the formalism began to break down. A 1939 assessment of federal departmental management, for example, noted the

> steadily growing realization that the task of leading great departments demands peculiar abilities, long trained and carefully organized. . . . The critical need, obviously, is to have men who, though working in a procedural atmosphere, have the initial gifts and the experience which prevent them from unduly subordinating substance to form . . . [who can cope with the fact that] that which is petty to the point of being laughable is mingled with the important, even the momentous. (MacMahon and Millett 1939, 10, 16)

Yet it was not until after World War II that the contemporary character of the departmental executive's role emerged fully and that a coherent understanding of that role began to develop. With the end of the war and the election of the first Republican Congress in sixteen years came renewed concern that government organizations be capably and efficiently administered.

The war had left behind a sprawling executive establishment and a national debt and federal budget of unprecedented size, and had weakened congressional control over the executive establishment. Congress was determined to achieve retrenchment, efficiency, and control (Emmerich 1971). In July 1947 Congress authorized creation of a Commission on Organization of the Executive Branch of the Government, which was to become known as the first Hoover Commission after its chairman, former President Herbert Hoover. The commission issued its report in 1949. It recommended that the department head be given authority to determine the organization within his department. He should be given authority to assign funds appropriated by the Congress for a given purpose to that agency in his department which he believes can best effect the will of Congress. (U.S. Commission 1949, 21)

Though postwar concern initially focused on the structure of departmental authority, attention soon turned to the problem of finding executives who could exercise it. The demands of the Korean War, the necessity for recruiting executive talent for the Eisenhower administration, the recognition that a large federal bureaucracy was a permanent feature of American life, and the general expansion of federal executive responsibility stimulated a major examination of high-level executives in the federal service, those whom the second Hoover Commission, created to study the personnel problems of government, termed "non-career executives" (U.S. Commission 1955).[5] Federal executive management received careful study throughout the 1950s and into the 1960s, especially by the Brookings Institution (Corson 1952; Lawton 1954; David and Pollock 1957; Bernstein 1958; Warner et al. 1963; Kilpatrick et al. 1964a, 1964b; Stanley 1964; Mann 1965; Stanley et al. 1967; Murphy et al. 1978).

Based on these studies, a coherent picture of the evolving character of the federal executive role emerged, and it was sobering.

In his 1958 study, *The Job of the Federal Executive,* Marver H. Bernstein, noting that "there is very little published information on what federal executives really do," reported the findings from a series of round-table discussions with two dozen distinguished political and career executives in the federal government.

Political appointees in department are usually inexperienced when they assume office and rarely stay long enough to maximize their effectiveness. They are the transient amateurs who are often inca-

5. The commission's principal recommendation concerning personnel was the creation of a Senior Career Service, an idea whose time was to await the administration of President Jimmy Carter and the passage of the Civil Service Reform Act of 1978.

pable of exerting firm control over the professional bureaucracy. (Bernstein 1958, 86)

The view of the senior federal executive as a "transient amateur," with limited authority, facing extraordinary demands, and finding it necessary to define his or her job has since been embellished and refined into a conventional wisdom.

In assessing how the American system of "separated institutions sharing power" circumscribes and shapes the power of the president, Richard E. Neustadt observed in 1960 that "the men who share in governing this country [i.e., the cabinet officers] frequently appear to act as though they were in business for themselves. So, in a real though not entire sense, they are and have to be" (Neustadt 1978, 23). Of federal executive departments, he observed that

> each has a separate statutory base; each has its statues to administer; each deals with a different set of subcommittees at the Capitol. Each has its own peculiar set of clients, friends, and enemies outside the formal government. Each has a different set of specialized careerists inside its own bailiwick. Our Constitution gives the President the 'take-care' clause and the appointive power. Our statues give him central budgeting and a degree of personnel control. All agency administrators are responsible to him. But they *also* are responsible to Congress, to their clients, to their staffs, and to themselves. In short, they have five masters. (Neustadt 1978, 107)

Three years later, a study of thousands of federal executives at various levels of responsibility produced the observation that for the executive functioning in the kind of system described by Neustadt,

> there is an Indian behind every tree. The executive cannot, however, in a fit of aggressive action simply go out and scalp the Indian. . . . To move aggressively, or even noisily, may invite undesirable or even disastrous attention from superordinates, opposite members, or the public at large. (Warner et al. 1963, 241–42)

Hugh Heclo (1977), noting that we still know little about the working world of top people in government, observed that "operations are based on craft knowledge—understanding acquired by learning on the job" (p. 3).

Another emergent line of thought concerned the behavior of government officials on the job, and their strategies of leadership, coping, and survival. Here, too, a rich imagery has evolved from the search for evocative metaphors to depict the personality types and styles of executive and bureaucratic behavior that one discovers in public life. In his *Inside Bureaucracy,* for example, Anthony Downs described five types of officials: climbers, who seek power and status; conservers, who are oriented to security and certainty; zealots, with narrow loyalties to sacred policies; advocates, who are broad-gauged zealots; and statesmen, with an altruistic orientation to the public interest (Downs 1967).[6] Based on interviews and test results, Sandra P. Schoenberg (1973) identified four leadership styles characteristic of public executives. The "innovator" is highly motivated and achievement oriented, with a taste for new ideas but not for the details of organization and follow-through. The "developer" is an innovator with endurance and an interest in future success. The "maintainer" has little interest in new programs but an ability to keep activities going, avoid conflict, and maintain good internal relations. The "figurehead" is a position filler whose only contribution may be to facilitate communications between constituents and political leaders.

Despite the emergence of these essentially descriptive, often highly stylized characterizations of the public executive, traditional public administration has remained far less concerned with the figure of the manager and more concerned with the ground of management: public laws, organizations, and functions. Thus public management cum the executive function in government is regarded within public administration as an emerging and distinct subfield or special focus.

In a 1983 review, Garson and Overman, based on an extensive survey of public management research in the United States, referred to "the increasing popularity of public management," perhaps, they suggest, because the term has more virile connotations than the term

6. Downs considers top-level executives as "quasipoliticians" rather than "officials."

administration (Garson and Overman 1983, 275). "Public management as a special focus of modern public administration is new" say Perry and Kraemer (1983), a view echoed by Rainey (1990, 157): "In the past two decades, the topic of public management has come forcefully onto the agenda of those interested in governmental administration," perhaps, he suggests, because of the growing unpopularity of government.

Rather than proclaim public management as something new, public administration scholars might well have claimed the opposite: that their field has "owned" the term for decades and that its progenitors were returning full circle to an earlier, perhaps more inspired, time. In 1940 an edited volume by one of public administration's important scholars and teachers, Fritz Morstein Marx, was titled *Public Management in the New Democracy* (Marx 1940). The journal of the International City Management Association has been named *Public Management* since the 1930s. A 1955 "classic" in public administration is Catheryn Seckler-Hudson's "Basic Concepts in the Study of Public Management" (1992).

Garson and Overman (1983) might well have been summarizing the views of the Morstein Marx volume when they defined public management as "an interdisciplinary study of the generic aspects of administration ... a blend of the planning, organizing, and controlling functions of management with the management of human, financial, physical, information and political resources" (p. 278). They cite six differences between public management thus conceived and public administration (thus also defining the field of public administration):

1. The inclusion of general management functions such as planning, organizing, control, and evaluation in lieu of discussion of social values and conflicts of bureaucracy and democracy;
2. An instrumental orientation favoring criteria of economy and efficiency in lieu of equity, responsiveness, or political salience;
3. A pragmatic focus on mid-level managers in lieu of the perspective of political or policy elites;
4. A tendency to consider management as generic, or at least

minimize the differences between public and private sectors in lieu of accentuating them;

5. A singular focus on the organization with external relations treated in the same rational manner as internal operations in lieu of a focus on laws, institutions and political bureaucratic processes;

6. A strong philosophical link with the scientific management tradition in lieu of close ties to political science or sociology. (Garson and Overman 1983, 278)

In defining public management, moreover, Perry and Kraemer (1983) claim their inspiration as Woodrow Wilson's famous 1887 essay. They summarize his foundations as "(1) government as the primary organizational setting, (2) the executive function as the proper focus, (3) the discovery of principles and techniques for more effective management as a key to developing administrative competence, and (4) comparison as a method for study and advancement of the field" (p. 1). Left unamended, this Wilsonian formulation might well serve as a charter for public management within the public policy community. But in updating these foundations, Perry and Kraemer subtly alter the second foundation, and identify themselves with public administration's domain, by insisting that "the focus of public management is on public administration as a profession and on the public manager as a practitioner of that profession, rather than as a politician or a statesman" (p. 5).

In their presumptively authoritative *Public Management: The Essential Readings,* Ott, Hyde, and Shafritz (1991) state:

> *Public management* is a major segment of the broader field of public administration.... Public management focuses on public administration as a profession and on the public manager as a practitioner of that profession.... Public management focuses on the managerial tools, techniques, knowledges, and skills that can be used to turn ideas and policy into programs of action. A few of these techniques and competencies are: position classification systems, recruitment and selection procedures, management by influence, budget analysis and formulation, supervisory skills, long

range or strategic planning, program and organizational evaluation, feedback and control mechanisms (typically through management information systems), contract management, project management, and reorganization. (p. 1)

Intellectual Foundations

Against the background of this field-defining literature, a more theoretical literature relating to the public executive function has emerged within public administration (Rainey 1989).

The foundation work is that of Herbert Simon, who, more than any other scholar, ended public administration's golden age within the academy. In a 1990 assessment of the most influential books in public administration in half a century, Simon's *Administrative Behavior* was "in a class by itself" (Sherwood 1990, 254).[7] Simon's behavioral approach to administration became the basis for a textbook entitled *Public Administration* he co-authored with Donald Smithburg and Victor Thompson, a 1950 book (and only the third public administration textbook) that was reissued with a new introduction in 1991.

In their introduction to the 1991 reissue, Simon and Thompson said that "*Public Administration* helped to redefine its field of study and practice by introducing [into a field traditionally preoccupied with organizational structure] two major new emphases; an emphasis upon human behavior and human relations in organizations, and an emphasis upon the interaction between administration and policy (including in the latter, politics)" (p. xiii). In assessing the value of the book, H. George Frederickson listed its principal themes as

> viewing the organization as a human enterprise that seeks both internal and external equilibrium, the debunking of the principles (the "proverbs") of administration as presented in the administrative management perspective, the concept of bounded rationality ("satisficing"), the widespread use of concepts from psychology, the importance of the context or setting of an organization to its func-

7. Bernard's *The Functions of the Executive* and Wildavsky's *The Politics of the Budgetary Process* were respectable also-rans.

tioning and its administrative practices ..., the insistence that understanding public organizations and administrative practices is a cumulative science or an administrative science, and, finally, the fact-value distinction. (Frederickson 1991, 77)

The authors' new introduction suggests that no intellectual departures have occurred since that would lead them to modify greatly their approach.

Yet the effort to determine public administration's most influential works found that there is widespread doubt within public administration that Simon's approach has had, or ought to have had, much of an impact on teaching, research, and practice. Following an attempt to assess the influence of Simon's *Administrative Behavior,* for example, Delmer Dunn concluded that POSDCORB "still reigns" and that Simon has apparently had little influence in creating a new paradigm" (Sherwood 1990, 253).

Moe (1991, 1994) makes the more complex argument that the formal concession that politics and administration are inseparable did not lead to the creation of a body of theory formally linking politics and administration. Instead, they became two separate fields of study that have had almost nothing to do with one another. "The great irony of modern public administration," Moe argues, "is that the politics-administration dichotomy never died, but in fact was institutionalized in the bifurcated structure of the new discipline.... Politics is understood in one way, organization in another" (p. 109). In Moe's judgment, no theory connecting politics and administration has emerged.

It was within the administration subfield of a bifurcated field that a focus on public management emerged.

Administration

Perhaps the first textbook avowing public *management* as its focus was Barry Bozeman's *Public Management and Policy Analysis* (1979). Bozeman's purpose was "conveying knowledge relevant to the management of complex organization[s]" (p. 2). Substantively, there was little to distinguish Bozeman's concept of public management from the traditional concerns of public administration other than a methodological note that his emphasis is on the "acquisition of strategic knowledge" (p. vi). Nevertheless, his elaboration of this notion is worth noting for its resonance with the current debate:

> I assume the public management should seek *rational* solutions, and by "rational" I mean to imply a respect for evidence and experience. We must not ... conclude that [we] can do no better than play hunches, follow ... intuition, or employ overly simple rules for decision making that reduce the quality of decisions even more than they reduce the complexity of the problems observed. ... [W]e can learn something from systematic inquiry and ... we can sometimes successfully apply our dearly won knowledge. (Bozeman 1979, vi)

A steady flow of comprehensive textbooks with management as their theme has appeared since Bozeman's book was published, most adopting the traditional approach that Bozeman found wanting. The following are illustrative.[8] *Managing the Public Organization* by Cole Blease Graham, Jr., and Steven W. Hays (1986) is dedicated to Luther Gulick and uses POSDCORB (adding E, for evaluation) as an organizing framework based on their belief that "the more effective public managers become in performing [these] administrative functions, the closer their agencies will come to fulfilling their basic objectives" (p. viii). Their discussion, published in 1986, is not at all mechanical or unsophisticated. "Administration," they insist, "cannot be divorced from politics" (p. 252). But they offer no integrated view of the executive function or public managerial roles. Their view is, if you are attending to the functions—using them as a checklist, if you will—you will come close to getting it right.

Steven Cohen's *The Effective Public Manager: Achieving Success in Government* (1988) is a handbook for the practice of public management written for "you," the practitioner. The effective public manager, he believes, must be an entrepreneur who is willing to take risks and assume personal responsibility for the consequences. The

---

8. Other early management-oriented textbooks include Gortner (1977), Starling (1982), and Klingner (1983).

effective public manager exhibits imagination and energy, a willingness to learn, a respect for others, and honesty in personal and professional relationships. "Every one of the problems that public managers face can be overcome," he believes. "Solutions ... always exist" (p. 6). Further, "any public manager can become an effective public manager" (p. 16).

Cohen's intellectual approach is experiential and inductive, both down-to-earth and reflective. Though he draws insights and ideas from a variety of literatures, his strong and optimistic convictions concerning issues of public management seem based primarily on participant observation, his own field of research, and frequent contact with public managers.

John Rehfuss's *The Job of the Public Manager* (1989) is concerned with public managers as career professionals who are accountable to legislators and chief executives. It is organized around themes of maintenance, representation, and planning, and chapters are concerned with goals and actors, decision making, politics, and the intergovernmental system. In its coverage, descriptive and synthetic approach, and expository tone, the book is similar to Cohen's *The Effective Public Manager,* though Rehfuss lacks Cohen's pungency and unquenchable optimism.

In *Public Management Strategies* (1990), Barry Bozeman and Jeffrey Straussman argue that "public management is the management of political authority" (p. xi). And "public management, like the earlier efforts in public administration [they refer to Woodrow Wilson, Leonard White, and Luther Gulick], requires a prescriptive approach" (p. xiii). The book is directed to "all public managers" and provides "some ideas, some clues, some arguments. We leave it to the public manager to sort out these ideas and to use his or her experience to adapt those worth adapting" (p. xiii).

The organization of this 1990 book is contemporary. It covers the political context of public management and the concept of strategy. Chapters are devoted to managing financial resources, marketing, managing information resources (strategically, of course), using organizational design and reorganization as strategic tools, and fostering innovation. In a concluding chapter, Bozeman and Straussman offer some refreshing points: effective public managers are good at self-assessment; effective strategic public managers (you can be effective and not strategic) are not boring people; and they have a sense of "the good" as well as "the politic." Above all, effective strategic public managers are patient. But they are also comfortable with analysis and analytic thinking, "so comfortable that he or she knows bogus analysis and will identify it as such, so comfortable that he or she will have a respect for analysis even when the analysis is counterintuitive" (p. 210).

"Public organizations perform crucial functions, and they need effective management," says Rainey in his comprehensive textbook *Understanding and Managing Public Organizations* (1991). (In contrast, the first substantive words in my own actor-focused book *Managing Public Policy* (1987) are "the jobs of the government's senior departmental executives are surprisingly difficult.") It is a sober, carefully documented text that begins with a discussion of "What Makes Public Organizations Distinctive" and concludes with a discussion of "Managing for Excellence in the Public Sector." Rainey's unit of analysis is, as noted, the organization; the book contains a useful appendix on "The Study of Organizations: A Historical Overview." His concluding chapter, however, turns finally to suggestions for the individual leader and manager. Some are crisp and straightforward and unexceptionable: "know the system," "establish effective relations between careerists and political officials," "prepare for politics." Some seem vacuous: "empower people," "prepare to manage complexity," "humanize public organizations." Assuming that such admonitions can be given specific meaning in specific contexts, they cannot be faulted for being misguided or wrong.

This brief survey of public management textbooks supports a number of observations. First, traditional public administration now incorporates an explicit concern for managerial roles and their effective performance. Second, though concern with extramural considerations varies, virtually all approaches to public management within public administration consider managerial roles within the intramural context of the people, functions, and structures of the organization, the field's traditional concerns. Third, description, classification, and synthesis are preferred to original analysis and argument. Fourth, and related to the third point, these expositions rely heavily on evidence and arguments from academic literature and only selectively, and usually for specific insights or reinforcements, on case material broadly construed. For this reason, the treatments often seem solid and careful but not terribly fresh, perceptive, or adventurous.

Bureaucracy

The study of bureaucracy, the other subfield within Moe's bifurcated profession, has also resulted in works that bear on the performance of the executive function in government. On the whole, these works are more academic than the previously cited textbooks. (But see Bendor [1994] for an evaluation of bureaucracy studies.)

Kenneth Meier's *Politics and the Bureaucracy: Policymaking in the Fourth Branch of Government* (1986) is a textbook that establishes as its problem the securing by society of a responsive and competent bureaucracy. In a separate paper published in 1989, he sets forth an approach to bureaucratic leadership, where leadership is viewed as "a series of strategic choices by members of the organization's dominant coalition" (p. 268). His conceptual framework is succinctly summarized as follows:

> The role of leadership in organizations is to acquire power for the organization. A leader's success in gaining resources and autonomy should determine, in part, the organization's ability to survive and achieve its policy goals. The actions of an organization's leaders can contribute to resources or autonomy by affecting any of three variables—cohesion, expertise, and clientele support. Cohesion is the degree of commitment that the organization's members have to the organization and its goals. Expertise is the specialized knowledge that an organization develops to use in the policy-making. (p. 269)

Meier goes on to outline a bureaucratic leader's strategic choices concerning membership inducements, policy objectives, implementation strategies, and coalitional strategies. Finally, he generates sixteen "testable hypotheses." For example, positive inducements will increase organizational cohesion whereas coercion and sanctions will reduce it; the more expertise possessed by the leader, the greater the influence over policy; the more competitors the organization's environment contains, the more crucial leadership decisions are to organizational survival.

Francis E. Rourke's *Bureaucracy, Politics, and Public Policy* (1984) is concerned with "the role of bureaucracy in the policy process . . . for it is in the crucible of administrative politics . . . that public policy is mainly hammered out, through bargaining, negotiation, and conflict among appointed rather than elected officials" (p. ix). Apart from an abstract and stylized discussion of "administrative discretion," however, the book devotes no attention to the executive role and its significance.

Jack H. Knott and Gary J. Miller's *Reforming Bureaucracy: The Politics of Institutional Choice* (1987) is also concerned with the social role of bureaucracy, but with a more analytically ambitious problem: to show how the institutions by which we govern ourselves are a product of self-interested behavior by political actors. Accordingly, "bureaucracy . . . [is] the understandable but inefficient result of reasonable actions by individuals with normal goals" (p. 11).

By advancing this rational choice perspective on bureaucracy in broad historical context, Knott and Miller mean to contend with two popular views: that bureaucracy is a product of stupidity and venality and that the design of administrative arrangements is a technical and nonpolitical problem. Following a brilliant analysis of the history of administrative reform in the United States, they conclude that "there is no structure whose neutrality, expertness, or other characteristics can automatically legitimize the policy choices it makes. . . . An institution is justified by its outcomes, rather than the other way around" (p. 274).

In his classic *Bureaucracy: What Government Agencies Do and Why They Do It* (1989), James Q. Wilson examines managers and executives within the context of the administrative state broadly construed. Executives in both government and business must be concerned with maintaining their organizations, he argues. But government executives, especially political appointees, are distracted by the fact that their success is not inexorably tied to the success of the organizations they manage. "The reputation of the secretary of state has little to do with his management of the Department of State" (p. 197).

Both political appointees and career executives, Wilson argues, must thoroughly understand the nature of the organizations they are maintaining and assure the sustained support of a constituency. Paradoxically, they gain an advantage in that their roles are so weakly defined. They have choices and the nature of their choices, and their success as executives, will reflect an interaction between their circumstances and their personalities. This idea originates in the work of Doig and Hargrove (1987), who deduced the importance of a match between skill and task by studying thirteen biographies of successful public officials. Other intellectual antecedents include Simon (1964) and James MacGregor Burns (1978), who, via different intellectual routes, argue that the extent of an executive's autonomy affects the scope for the exertion of personal influence on events.

Much of Wilson's insight into executives' roles and contributions employs an elaborated notion of an interaction between the two independent influences: circumstances and personalities. He classifies types of circumstances and styles of executive action: coping agencies, production agencies, craft organizations, and procedural organizations; advocates, budget cutters, decision makers, and negotiators. Obviously, some "fits" are better than others. A good fit is one in which an executive uses his or her autonomy to mobilize constituencies on behalf of objectives in such a way as to reconcile the pursuit of personal reputation with effectiveness at enhancing organizational performance.

Borrowed Ideas

That nontraditional scholarship can thrive in a field as broad and diverse as public administration is not surprising. Of particular interest is the fact that ideas orphaned in the public policy community often flourish in public administration. Concern with implementation, for example, has faded in the public policy community (see p. 57) but retains its vigor in public administration.

The most widely cited work is Sabatier and Mazmanian (1980). In a fashion public policy types would claim is typical of atheoretical public administration, Sabatier and Mazmanian present a flow diagram of the variables involved in the implementation process. The variables are classified as those "independent variables" affecting "the tractability of the problem," "the ability of statute to favorably structure the implementation process, and political variables affecting support for statutory objectives. The interaction among them is made manifest in "the stages of implementation," which are termed "dependent variables" (p. 541).

Other public administration scholars express considerable dissatisfaction with the state of this subfield. Helen Ingram says, for example, "the field of implementation has not yet achieved conceptual clarity" (1990, 462). Her review of the literature leads her to conclude that "implementation studies would profit from a broad, flexible framework that synthesizes and orders the insights of the large implementation literature" (pp. 470–71). She suggests a framework that represents a considerable improvement in analytic sophistication over that of Sabatier and Mazmanian.

Ingram develops a typology of statutes based on whether (1) information costs and (2) negotiation costs incurred by the legislature are low or high. If information costs are low, she argues, statutes allow for procedural flexibility. If negotiation costs are low, statutes incorporate clear and specific goals. By this logic, if both costs are high, the resulting statutes have open-ended goals but tight procedural constraints.

Each statute is associated with an "appropriate approach." If both types of costs are low, a command-and-control, highly programmed approach is appropriate. The achievement of goals is the appropriate criterion for evaluation. The critical variables affecting implementation will include changes in exogenous circumstances. If both types of costs are high, implementation will be associated with continuous bargaining. The appropriate evaluation criteria include whether the resulting program has earned broad agreement and support. The critical variable affecting implementation is the dynamics of client group relations.

A similarly motivated but sharply contrasting "third generation" approach to implementation studies is that of Malcolm L. Goggin and his colleagues (1990). "At the center of this new 'third-generation' scholarship," they argue, "is an emphasis on conceptual clarification, and the careful operationalization and measurement of variables; equally important is a set of policy analytical techniques that are both comparative and longitudinal" (p. 195). They recommend a research design that "combines content analysis (if properly administered, a method strong on reliability) with elite interviews ... and the careful administration of a mail questionnaire, procedures that, in combination, can tap aspects of implementation dynamics and assist in establishing validity" (p. 196).

In their comprehensive analysis of the field of implementation scholarship, Barry M. Mitnick and Robert W. Backoff (1984), in yet another approach, argue that

> public policy implementation can be understood as a time-varying system of *implementation relations* between potential principals and implementing agents. Those relations are driven by the *incentive relations* at their cores; the problems observed in implementation can therefore often be analyzed in terms of *incentive failures*. (pp. 113–14; italics in original)

Their attempt to construct an "incentive system model" quickly gets out of hand, however, and produces a wiring diagram of Gordian complexity. Nevertheless, their insistence on viewing implementation in terms of analytically derived relations, instead of what they call "atomistic factors like resource scarcity, environmental complexity, or goal clarity," leads to many useful insights of potential value in applied work.

Finally, and in another sharp contrast, Laurence J. O'Toole, Jr. (1991) explores limitations and possibilities for rational choice contributions to the study of policy implementation. His assessment of the field is that "a great deal of what passes for conventional wisdom among scholars about policy implementation has a proverbial character; it consists of overly broad assertions regarding how to achieve implementation success, is only loosely connected to coherent bodies of carefully specified theory, and is internally contradictory.... Too often promising ideas have gone largely unresearched while highly questionable ones have persisted despite the presence of contravening evidence" (pp. 2, 4).

O'Toole goes on to observe that "to the extent that scholarship on policy implementation is conducted by specialists in public administration, the approaches can be expected to be heavily empirical and inductive and to borrow relatively little from such fields as game theory and formal network analysis" (p. 10). His own efforts to draw on such fields is on behalf of his interest in multiactor, nonhierarchical implementation processes characteristic of most policies implemented through our intergovernmental system. He argues:

> Among the features of an implementation setting that might be productively treated in simple but formal fashion are: the impact of altering policy characteristics on various types of multiorganizational arrangements; the results on cooperation of increases in levels of trust through the whole or a part of a multiactor setting; the effects of iteration in different implementation settings; the effect of such potentially important items as different levels of information, alternative monitoring systems, different payoffs, contrasting facilitative efforts, varying numbers of actors, alternative structures of interdependence, different discount rates, other agendas (that is, connected games), the relative presence and prominence of mediating interest associations (for groups of public or private actors), varying assumptions about the possibility of side payments, different institutional rules regarding such issues as vetoes, and contrasting initial states, all on the likelihood of cooperation. (p. 37)

But he cautions that "the complexity and fluidity of the typical less-than-institutionalized implementation arena, especially during the interesting formative period, impose constraints on what can be expected from such approaches. Game theorists, for instance, may find that situations of great interest to empirical researchers cannot be modelled, let alone solved" (p. 37). This caveat notwithstanding, O'Toole insists that "rigorous thinking and careful representation of some of the more important questions of implementation are clearly needed" (p. 38).

Another public management idea that could be said to have originated in the public policy community only to fade there (with exceptions such as Weiss's work, cited below) while thriving in public administration is the "tools" approach.

Within the public policy community, Eugene Bardach, Richard Elmore, and Lester Salamon made important early contributions to the subject. In *The Implementation Game* (1977), Bardach identified four generic techniques or social technologies: prescription, enabling, positive incentives, and deterrence. In a later paper, Elmore (1986) took a similar approach, identifying such generic tools as mandates, inducements, and system alterations. Such tools, these authors argue, have different behavioral implications.

In a seminal paper, Salamon (1981) argued that the rise of what he called "third-party government," or the substitution of performance contracts for employment contracts in securing the provision of public goods, has changed "the forms of government action." These forms include loans, loan guarantees, new forms of regulation, tax subsidies, government corporations, interest subsidies, insurance, and the like. Salamon proposed a formal analytic approach to appraising their implications for public policy, hypotheses that are subject to disconfirmation, including what he called "The Public Management Paradox": ". . . the types of instruments that are the easiest to implement may be the hardest to enact; conversely, the forms that are most likely to be enacted are also the most difficult to carry out" (p. 272).

Within public administration, the tools approach has been pursued with two different emphases. Anne Schneider and Helen Ingram (1991) are concerned with what they term the behavioral (as opposed to the administrative) implications of tools. They begin with the assumption that "public policy almost always attempts to get [or enable] people to do things that they might not otherwise do" (p. 513). There are four reasons why people may not act as we wish:

> They may believe the law does not direct them or authorize them to take action; they may lack incentives or capacity to take the actions needed; they may disagree with the values implicit in the means or ends; or the situation may involve such high levels of uncertainty that the nature of the problem is not known, and it is unclear what people should do or how they might be motivated. (p. 514)

Policy tools address these problems "by providing authority, incentives, or capacity, by using symbolic and hortatory proclamation to influence perceptions or values, or by promoting learning to reduced uncertainty" (p. 514). Their argument is that research on policy design and implementation must recognize these behavior dimensions of various policy tools.

Linder and Peters (1989) take a very different view. They argue that "the received view is that theory development can best proceed inductively by generating contingency statements from case materials that illustrate the application of different instruments to policy problems" (p. 53). The "ontological assumptions" underlying this approach were that context determined performance and that interventions should be fitted to contexts. Their contrasting approach is to ground theory construction on "policymakers' own views of what makes instruments operationally and symbolically comparable or unique" even though "they "may not have much of a theoretical basis or elaborate dimensionality" (p. 56). Policy choice, they argue, is far less often based on a rational/analytic grasp of appropriateness than on "subjective elements" (p. 56).

The Public Interest

For all its instrumental emphasis, public administration is also prone to embrace normative imperatives associated with a constitutionally grounded concept of the public interest. It is well and good to focus on the performance of executives, the performance of organizations, and the achievement of public policy objectives and to attempt to bring them into balance. Though broad, this domain may nonetheless be too limiting to both theorists and practitioners.

The primary concern, some public administration scholars argue, ought to be with the performance of the polity, with citizen roles and performance, and with the public administrator's role in creating and sustaining relationships between citizens and their governing institutions. Many scholars in public administration—and, as we later see, in public policy and elsewhere—have insisted that administration is essentially about serving the public interest.

Gary Wamsley (1990) has argued, for example, that there is a need for identifying the public administrator's "unique claims for a special role in governance" (p. 115). He enumerates these claims as follows:

1. expertise in operationalizing policy in the form of specific programs;
2. expertise in creating and sustaining processes and dialogue that results in the broadest possible definition of the public interest;
3. skills in community-building politics and the fostering of active citizenship;
4. guardianship ... of the Constitution and constitutional processes. (pp. 114–15)

Wamsley's metatheme is that all skill and expertise should be exercised on behalf of "the public interest and the common good" (p. 154). He urges scholars to "build upon the descriptive-explanatory approach to theory-building derived from organization theory but use the insights we gain to develop (in the tradition of political theory) a normative concept and prescribe a social construct that has significance for the state and the values that surround" (p. 128).

In John Rohr's view (1986) "the Public Administration" is, on the one hand, subordinate but, on the other hand, necessarily imbued with an exalted purpose: "to uphold the Constitution of the United States.... Administrators should use their discretionary power in order to maintain the constitutional balance of powers in support of individual rights" (p. 181). By sustaining an appropriate balance between constitutional subordination and autonomy, "we can transform erstwhile lackeys, leakers, obstructionists, and whistle blowers into administrative statesmen" (p. 183).

Robert Denhardt (1993) is similarly attentive to moral imperatives. "A sense of moral vision is exactly what is required of all organizations in the future. Public organizations are and indeed must be permeated with a commitment to values, not merely values that reinforce self-serving behavior but values that relate to the concepts of freedom, justice and the public interest" (p. 20). His five principles of public management begin with "a commitment to values," by which he means a subordination of structural concerns to "professionalism and integrity, service and quality" (p. 21).

H. George Frederickson (1994) has made perhaps the most inclusive and the most specific normative statement concerning the nature of what he terms "the soul of public administration." Public administration must, he argues, define its domain broadly but at the same time limit the scope of the field to the implementation of policy and to the nonpartisan advocacy of "the mission of our organizations." He defines the essential tasks of the field to be efficiency, economy, and equity in the management of public agencies done in such a way as to "enhance the prospects for change and responsiveness." A field so inspired will, he believes, be immune to the distractions of partisan politics and to "promoters and hustlers" of fashionable precepts, relying instead on the "best thinking and the most effective applications" of reliable theories and concepts.

Public administration, then, offers a sweeping menu of approaches to the subject of public management, from the institutional/descriptive to the formally analytic to the didactic. But the fact that the unit of analysis remains the bureau, the organization, or the institution, all viewed within a public law framework, has left room for an aggressive group of nouveau scholars and teachers whose loyalties are to policy, to outcomes, and to entrepreneurship, and to the kind of scholarship that will serve these objectives.

3

THE PUBLIC MANAGER
AS POLICYMAKER

"But tell me how she set about it!"
"There's no theory in that profession; only practice. . . ."
— Honoré de Balzac

In the past two decades, a small group of scholars in the new public policy programs has devoted increasing attention to the leadership and direction of public agencies. Owing to their efforts, public management, defined more or less as the executive function in government, has moved from the background to the foreground of scholarship and practice in these programs.

In the beginning, these scholars and teachers had much intellectual capital to draw on. Traditional public administration, as the preceding chapter makes clear, produced classic works and important traditions of inquiry, including the early work of Herbert Simon, the Brookings studies of government executives, and teaching cases concerned with management and decision making. The study of public bureaucracies was a recognized subfield of both sociology and political science. The new programs explicitly rejected these traditions, however, and sought to create a teaching and intellectual enterprise that was distinctive and new.

Public Management as Policy Leadership

Taking their cue from the success of quantitatively trained systems analysts in the management of national security programs (and some glimmerings of potential success in social programs), founding faculties of public policy programs sought to attract students interested in "high policy" rather than in careers as functionaries in the civil service. The idea was to give them rigorous training in the analytic skills that seemed to be in growing demand by the "best and brightest" public officials.

The public policy schools rejected traditional public administration as a source of insights into this mission for several reasons. Traditional public administration, according to Donald Stokes, was viewed as descriptive rather than prescriptive, preoccupied by institutions rather than by choice and action, and insufficiently interdisciplinary (Stokes 1986). Joel Fleishman (1990) refers to "the desultory background of existing programs in public administration" (p. 736). Richard Elmore (1986) argues that public administration was "a collection of discrete and unrelated subjects in search of an intellectual focus, preoccupied with institutional description rather than analysis, and lacking in sufficient intellectual rigor to command the respect of other academic disciplines or the public at large" (p. 70).[1]

A new approach to education for the new breed of public servants was needed. "Perhaps the most exciting idea which animated the new public policy schools," says Fleishman, "was the opportunity to focus not on the means whereby government acts but on the ends to which government power may be put" (1990, 737). "Wanting to soar high in the company of faculty from very high-flying fields" (Stokes 1986), they would build on "the prestige of quantitative analysis" to train people with, as Elmore puts it, "an analytic

---

1. Two books that depict the essence of the public administration that was being rejected are Mosher (1968) and Mosher, ed. (1975). It is of interest to note that Dwight Waldo, writing in the latter volume about "Education for Public Administration in the Seventies," took no notice of the emergent influence of public policy analysis on education for public administration, even though a more prescient article by Don K. Price, the founding dean of the Kennedy School of Government, followed his.

frame of mind" (1986, 70), decision-driven and prescriptive, "Ptolemaic" in Stokes's term, rather than "Copernican."

Though the emphasis in the new curriculums was on the quantitative skills needed to evaluate policies, political and organizational analysis was from the outset regarded as essential to, as Stokes puts it, plug "the adoption gap," that is, the gap between policy adoption and end result, and its place in the new curriculums was assured (Hargrove 1975). It was from this patch of curricular ground that the field of public management was to grow.

According to Elmore, "The new public management has its intellectual roots in policy analysis [and in the discipline of economics], albeit on the political and organizational side of the field" (1986, 72). The primary concern, reflected in Elmore's own work as well as in the seminal work of the Berkeley School (Eugene Bardach, Jeffrey Pressman, Aaron Wildavsky), was with what was coming to be termed "the implementation problem." The question was, How can policy ideas be translated into the operating results of governments? Nevertheless, says Stokes, anticipating Terry Moe's (1991) complaints about public administration, "As long as political analysis was cast primarily in the role of plugging the 'adoption' and 'implementation' gaps, the link [between political thinking and public management] was less prominent" (1986, 55). The early courses were largely descriptive and passive, proposing no theoretical links between politics and policymaking. An "evolutionary refinement" in the curriculum, as Fleishman (1990) puts it, was needed.

Fleishman sees development of the current focus of public management as originating in Mark Moore's efforts to "refocus political and organizational analysis into prescriptive subject matter, with a point of view that is decidedly strategic" (1990, 743). The important innovation, Fleishman says, was Moore's design of a course on "upward and outward" management called Political Management and Institutional Leadership.

> In "political management," perhaps more than in any other course, ... the spirit of the Public Policy schools, that which most dramatically differentiates it from public administration, comes through most strikingly.... By teaching skills in the context of decision-

forcing cases within courses characterized by a uniformly strategic orientation, premised on utilizing sophisticated analytic techniques, the Public Policy schools seem to me to be in no danger of relapsing into the old public administration mold (1990, 745–46).

Observes Stokes: "[S]trategic political thinking sets off the public manager who is able to *move* an agency from one who plays a custodial role.... [T]he strategic manager sees the small openings presented by the agency's routine to induce change toward an identified goal, step by step, as the deep sea fisherman lands the fish in the occasional moments when the line is slack. Imparting this outlook to future managers is as challenging a task as any that faces the policy curriculum" (1986, 55).

The emphasis on strategic public management in policy curriculums evolved into a focus on the practice of the general management function. In 1979, Graham Allison argued that "the general management functions concentrated in the CEO of a private business are, by constitutional design, spread in the public sector among a number of competing institutions and thus shared by a number of individuals whose ambitions are set against one another" (p. 33). Improvements in public management will come, Allison said, from "an articulation of the general management function and a self-consciousness about the general public management point of view" (p. 37). "The effort to develop public management as a field of knowledge should start from problems faced by practicing public managers" (p. 38).

By 1984, Moore summarized the emerging state of the art: "Our conception of 'public management' adds responsibility for goal setting and political management to the traditional responsibilities of public administration.... Our conception of public management adds some quintessential executive functions such as setting purpose, maintaining credibility with overseers, marshalling authority and resources, and positioning one's organization in a given political environment as central components of a public manager's job" (Moore 1984, 2, 3). The gist of public management is "conceiving and implementing public policies that realize the potential of a given political and institutional setting" (p. 3).

This emphasis, as Moore saw it, is in contrast to the traditional approach, which he characterized as "developing efficient, programmatic means for accomplishing well defined policy goals," maintaining fiduciary accountability, and exemplifying the value of neutral competence. Steven Kelman (1987) articulated the mission of professional schools of public policy and management more concisely, and with clear jurisdictional implications, as contributing to "the growth of a public management professional culture" (p. 281).

Concerning this emerging orthodoxy, there have been a few contrary voices and some useful controversies. Aaron Wildavsky (1985) long doubted that much is new. "By substituting one word, namely, 'administration' for 'management,' the old world of public administration is being revived under the new rubric of 'public management'" (p. 33). Wildavsky saw the effort not as original but as both an effort to imitate business schools and a quest for "conceptual hegemony," a reaction against the limits placed on policy analysts by the realities of political and organizational life. J. Patrick Dobel (1992) makes a sardonic reference to "the ongoing effort to create a new 'myth' for public management. The public management movement purportedly distanced itself from public administration by emphasizing a political and activist orientation—heroes and entrepreneurs became the stock and trade of its case studies," at the expense of institutions (1992, 147). According to Wildavsky, public management is public administration; according to Dobel, it is hero worship.

These voices notwithstanding, founding a field on "the executive in government" making the most of an opportunity is a decisive break from traditional public administration. It identifies the field with a particular kind of actor rather than with institutions or functions, and an actor without explicit constitutional sanction at that. Within a professional school context, this choice of emphasis leads almost inexorably to a proactive, even transcendent, view of that actor's role. A passive, descriptive, noncommittal social science, and a Wilsonian (both James Q. and Woodrow) view of the executive role as maintenance, holds few seductions for teachers and scholars whose ambition is to train and advise the leaders of public policy.

The New Practice of Scholarship

Even if traditional public administration was rejected as a source of knowledge, founding faculties had their own intellectual capital to draw on. In the "precolumbian" literature that was the intellectual heritage of the new schools of public policy, it was Richard Neustadt who was most influential, at least on the East Coast. His *Presidential Power* (1978) offered, as Stokes put it, "a prudential theory of the exercise of power by a central political actor that depends on a number of shrewdly observed factual generalizations" (Stokes 1986, 48). Its central insight, "Executive power is the power to persuade," has become a defining aphorism for public management. In contrast, Thomas Schelling's *The Strategy of Conflict* (1960) was apparently regarded as too abstract and remote from managerial concerns. Wildavsky's *The Politics of the Budgetary Process* (1964) was too pessimistic, noninterventionist, and critical of the analytic arts to be influential much beyond the West Coast.

The first sustained work of scholarship emerging from the new schools was Allison's *Essence of Decision* (1971). Though not identified as such, it was fundamentally concerned with organizational and political analysis and, by implication, with public management. Shortly, other contributions by young scholars from the new schools began to appear: Bardach's *The Skill Factor in Politics* (1972), Pressman and Wildavsky's *Implementation* (1973), and Steinbruner's *The Cybernetic Theory of Decision* (1974). All were concerned with political and organizational analysis, not policy analysis, the quantitative discipline that lay at the heart of the new schools.

Essence of Decision is an intellectual achievement owing much to the author's participation in the newly formed Kennedy School's interdisciplinary Research Seminar on Bureaucracy, Politics, and Policy. Drawing on the emergent literature of organization theory (but unduly equating that theory with the ideas of the Carnegie School [Moe 1991]), Allison distilled three distinct models of "bureaucratic choice"—rational actor, organizational process, and governmental politics—and serially applied the logic of each to a single case, the Cuban Missile Crisis, to show how each contributed to interpreting the data in the case.

The models themselves are of continuing intellectual interest

(Bendor and Hammond 1989, 1992). But the book also contained two potentially powerful methodological ideas. The first was Allison's avowed intention of producing scholarly work that would appeal both to "artists" and "scientists," to produce both "explanations" (i.e., the art) and "concepts and propositions in terms of which explanations are produced" (i.e., the science) (p. vi). An equally important idea was the value Allison placed on formulating and evaluating alternative, controvertible explanations for political events. Further, in an important aside, Allison cautioned that the essence of any decision may still remain impenetrable to the observer. Thus craftsmanship, analysis, and humility should be, intentionally, the distinguishing characteristics of this new work.

Steinbruner's *The Cybernetic Theory of Decision* (1974), the product of the same Harvard intellectual environment, is an exceedingly erudite book. In a spirit similar to that of Allison, Steinbruner probed the literatures bearing on decision making, with a special focus on the notion of "bounded rationality," and synthesized a variety of contributions into two distinct paradigms, which he labeled "analytic" and "cybernetic." According to the latter, and in sharp contrast to the value-integrating assumptions of the former,

> the decision process is organized around the problem of controlling inherent uncertainty by means of highly focused attention and highly programmed response. . . . At the level of collective decisions the paradigm posits a process in which decisions are fragmented into small segments and the segments treated sequentially. The process is dominated by established procedure. (Steinbruner 1974, 86–87)

The potential importance of this idea for managerial behavior is clear enough. Steinbruner himself concludes that

> in a world of great complexity and poorly developed knowledge, it is inherently easier to develop negative arguments than to advance constructive ones. Uncertainty naturally allies with doubt, hesitation, and delay. Fully warned Presidents are likely to vacillate under counteracting pressures; their governments are likely to act incoherently. (p. 333)

He notes the dilemma of the conflicting implications of "giving warning" and "giving confidence" to executives. Also of interest are his observations on the implications for applied research of drawing paradigm distinctions. Steinbruner's book, like Allison's, is based on evidence from a detailed case study. In such applied work, Steinbruner says, "very high standards ought to obtain ... in actual application of the paradigms, the important dimensions of complexity must be laid forth, facts must be well documented, and care must be taken to apply the separate perspectives fairly and independently" (p. 150).[2]

Of an altogether different concern were the new intellectual contributions from the West Coast.

Pressman and Wildavsky's *Implementation* (1973) virtually launched the field of implementation research. Implementation begins, the authors argue, when a program has been created through legislative and administrative decisions. "Implementation ... is the ability to forge subsequent links in the causal chain so as to obtain the desired results.... The longer the chain of causality, the more numerous the reciprocal relationships among the links and the more complex implementation becomes" (pp. xxiii–xxiv). Their objective in undertaking a study of the Economic Development Administration's employment program in Oakland, California, was, in keeping with the professional mission of the new schools, to improve governmental performance: "By concentrating on the implementation of programs, as well as their initiation, we should be able to increase the probability that policy promises will be realized" (p. 6). Thus,

2. Robert F. Coulam's *Illusions of Choice* (1977) applied the Allison/Steinbruner analytic framework to the U.S. Department of Defense decision to acquire the F-111 and concluded: "The F-111 program confirms that a powerful body of theory is presently available for conceptualizing the implementation problem and, more generally, for understanding the behavior of large public organizations.... [T]he cybernetic paradigm significantly broadens our understanding, as it powerfully evokes the rigidities, the narrow vision, the objectively strange assumptions that, even casual observation informs us, suffuse much of the activity of large organizations" (pp. 363, 366).

their focus on implementation called attention to how the entire governmental system, from federal to local, functioned on behalf of policy achievement.

The problem with the Pressman-Wildavsky approach, in Eugene Bardach's view, was that it did not go beyond suggestive typologies to get at underlying processes of implementation. Bardach's *The Implementation Game* (1977) is based on a case study of mental health reform policymaking in California and about a powerful and successful political entrepreneur in the California legislature. "The essential implementation problem," Bardach argues, "is to control and direct the vast profusion of program-related activities carried on by numerous and disparate organizations and individuals so as to achieve program objectives, keep costs down, and reduce delay." He chose the "master metaphor" of games to characterize these processes. This metaphor

> directs us to look at the players, what they regard as the stakes, their strategies and tactics, their resources for playing, the rules of play (which stipulate the conditions for winning), the rules of "fair" play (which stipulate the boundaries beyond which lie fraud or illegitimacy), the nature of the communications (or lack of them) among the players, and the degree of uncertainty surrounding the possible outcomes. (p. 56)

His purpose, too, was to "render practical advice" to political actors caught up in implementation games.

Bardach's conclusions convey a rather profound pessimism about policy making and public management.

> Top political appointees in the executive branch need a long time to master the details of what is actually happening in implementation games. By the time they have mastered the details, they are almost ready to leave. In any case, it often happens that their incentives are to indulge more in rhetoric and self-display than to pursue the unglamorous tasks of cajoling, pushing, threatening, and so on. (p. 280)

But perhaps they should not try. "Markets and mores are sturdier and more sensible, and government is probably less sensible and less reliable, than liberal reformers have been willing to admit.... [I]t is ... essential to become more modest in our demands on, and expectations of, the institutions of representative government" (p. 283). Moreover—and this constituted a potential mandate for scholarship—the most important problems that affect public policy are almost surely not those of implementation but those of basic political, economic, and social theory."

Reacting to intellectual shortcomings in the emerging field of implementation research, and to the pessimism at Berkeley, Richard Elmore articulated (acknowledging an original idea of Mark Moore) a metaphorical concept that continues to influence public management: backward mapping. "Backward mapping," Elmore argued, "explicitly questions the assumption that policymakers ought to, or do, exercise the determinant influence over what happens in the implementation process" (Elmore 1979–80, 604). Backward mapping begins with "a relatively precise target at the lowest level of the system" and defines the capacities and resources needed to meet it. The implication for public management is clear enough: "the problem-solving ability of complex systems depends not on hierarchical control but on maximizing discretion at the point where the problem is most immediate." (p. 605)

Success at backward mapping, Elmore insists, requires a rather deep grasp of "how to use the structure and process of organizations to elaborate, specify, and define policies." (p. 606) He sees the approaches of economists who advocate marketlike incentives as a substitute for organizational pathologies as antithetical to this goal. "The implementation literature," he argues, provides strong support for an analytic framework that takes account of reciprocity in the relationship between superiors and subordinates in organizations, the connection between hierarchical control and increased complexity, discretion as an adaptive device, and bargaining as a precondition for local effect." (p. 611)

Elmore's methodological observations are as interesting as the idea itself. In his view, advice based on implementation studies was "desultory and strategically vague" because the cases on which they were based did not support more than cautious, incremental findings. He urged implementation researchers to have more "nerve," to use and take greater liberties with the literature. "The important issue," Elmore argued, "is not whether the framework of analysis is 'right' or 'wrong' but whether it is sufficiently clear to be controvertible. It is less important to agree on a single framework for analyzing implementation problems than it is to be clear about the consequences of adopting one framework over another." (p. 602)

On the whole, this early scholarship suggests that the new public policy schools represented exciting, interdisciplinary environments in which the conceptual and research tools of the disciplines were selectively being brought to bear on the raw material of significant public problems. While the in-depth case study became *de rigueur,* so was a scholarly disposition toward data from the field.

The approaches to selectivity by the early public policy scholars were themselves significant. Preference for concepts such as bounded rationality and bureaucratic politics signaled the rejection of economic theory as a basis for understanding public management in favor of models that comprehended the complex operating realities of public bureaucracies in specific political contexts and the complex operations of the human mind under the pressure of events.

The intellectual goal of the new schools, if their literature is any indication, was the balancing of art and science and the production of insights of considerable subtlety and depth. Contributors to the literature took issue with one another, and insights were cumulative: Allison-Steinbruner-Coulam; Pressman/Wildavsky-Bardach-Elmore. As an academic field, public policy studies in general and public management in particular showed considerable intellectual originality and promise.

The New Scholarship for Practice

A new form of scholarly work was also becoming popular in these programs. The motivating belief was that a closer existential relationship to the world of practice would enable the new schools to contribute more effectively to it. The idea was to get close to practitioners, learn what they know, and make practitioner skill and wisdom accessible to students.

The idea of learning by observing and documenting actual contexts and cases found a natural application in adaptations of the case method of teaching to the new schools' teaching mission. Cases had long been in use in public administration programs, many emphasizing decision making, the new schools' apparent forte (Stein 1952).[3] Public policy schools were impressed more by the uses of cases in business schools in fields such as business policy and decision making. Under Neustadt's patronage, an ambitious case program was created at the Kennedy School. In 1978, Joseph Bower and Charles Christenson, faculty members at the Harvard Business School, produced the first casebook for use in the new schools, *Public Management: Text and Cases* (1978). (My own casebook appeared two years later.)

Articles on public management for practitioners in both public and private sectors began appearing in the *Harvard Business Review*. In "Finding Where the Power Lies in Government," Dan H. Fenn, Jr., a former public official and instructor at the Harvard Business School, argued that those with a stake in government performance need "some map, albeit crude, of the policy process.... Who are the chief actors? What are their concerns, clout, and constituencies? What kind of a proposal (using common goals) can I put together that will have the best chance of working?" (Fenn 1979, 152). Contrary to conventional wisdom, he argued that the business of government is nonhierarchical with many actors, each of whom can be placed at the center of a power network. Bower's 1977 article on "Effective Public Management" contained the deservedly famous sentence: "It is almost true that the business executive's enabling resources—structure and people—are the public executive's constraints" (p. 134) and illustrated his meaning with material drawn

---

3. A public administration casebook, *Cases in Public Management*, published in 1973 with a second edition in 1978, was unknown in the public policy schools (Golembiewski and White 1978). I recall that in my first year on the Kennedy School faculty, Don K. Price, the school's first dean, handed me his tattered copy of Stein and suggested, in his courtly way, that public administration was not all that backward. I still have that volume.

from teaching cases. The same year, Lynn and Seidl in the *Harvard Business Review* published "'Bottom-line' Management for Public Agencies" based on their experiences in the management of federal agencies (1977).

The notion gained popularity that an understanding of public management would be advanced by continuous dialogue between faculty and practitioners, indeed, by breaking down the distinction between the two. Practitioner-scholars—faculty who combined governmental experience with scholarly interests—were eagerly sought. This hybrid concept was extended to include practitioner-teachers; first Gordon Chase, following a long career in government, and then former Massachusetts Governor Michael S. Dukakis, for example, became full-time faculty members at the Kennedy School and were central figures in its emerging public management emphasis.

By the mid-1970s, practitioner wisdom such as Donald Rumsfeld's "rules" for presidential advisers was in circulation, to be followed shortly by Gordon Chase's "Bromides for Public Managers" (1980). The latter, which would become the basis for a book (Chase and Reveal 1983) that appeared after Chase's death in 1980, were down to earth, anecdotal, and didactic: "Obtain and maintain the support of the political boss"; "make sure the money is there"; "make use of (or neutralize if need be) those outside of government whom you don't control" (Chase 1980, 14). Chase believed public management was an art, not a science. He was described by colleagues as the prototypical "reflective practitioner" (Chase and Reveal 1983).

Two works exemplify the new practice-driven scholarship. Martha Weinberg's *Managing the State* (1977) "grew out of my experience working in executive offices in two states" (p. ix). The practitioner influence on her research is evident in her orientation: "though the study is not written from the perspective of the journalist, the business executive, the politician, or the constituent, it relies heavily on the insights and cautions characteristic of each" (p. 6).

Though Weinberg invokes both the "rational actor" and "muddling through" models of executive decision making, her versions of the models are caricatures. The conceptual development and relevance of such models is not her concern. "To understand the dynamics of executive leadership, it is necessary to raise the level of argument beyond considering which of the two models is more correct and to ask what executives consider when they make specific decisions." She concludes that "the single most important factor both the models . . . fail to take into account is the importance of crisis in determining how a governor manages. . . . The important question to ask about a political executive's management is, therefore, what dictates what a crisis is and, more particularly, how this affects a governor's dealings with his agencies" (p. 218).

In 1979 Chase published his classic paper "Implementing a Human Services Program: How Hard Will It Be?" In it, Chase identified *ex post* forty-four obstacles that had hampered his ability to implement programs while he was administrator of New York City's Health Services Administration. "Not until some time later," he said, did he realize that these obstacles could have been anticipated. This realization led him to convert the obstacles to a typology of precepts that could be applied *ex ante*, in effect a protocol for backward mapping. Applying the precepts retrospectively to three programs he had attempted to implement, he showed how their prospective use might have enabled him to manage more effectively and set priorities more wisely.

Chase's implementation framework, far more than his "bromides," seemed to stimulate the hope that practice-driven theory could add insight and prescriptive power to the study of public management in a way that scholarship conforming to traditional academic standards could not.

The "What Counts?" Literature

As the new public policy schools entered their second decade, the focus on public management sharpened, and intellectual products were more numerous and more diverse. Though there was little coalescence around themes or issues, two distinguishable orientations began to emerge, one more ptolemaic and centered on the executive as a biographically specific actor with political influence, the other more copernican and centered on executives and managers as role players in a complex, open system explicitly involving organizations and institutions. Both concepts were in some tension with the founding notion of the public executive as achieving influence through reliance on formal policy analysis.

The underlying intellectual issues surfaced most clearly during a 1988 symposium featuring a debate about "What counts?" in achieving the goals of public policy? (For a summary, see Sawhill 1989.) Though a specific occasion at which proponents for policy analysis, organization, and leadership argued their case, the symposium breached an ongoing, if implicit, debate in the literature. In particular, the underlying tension between leadership and organization as decisive in policy outcomes accounts for much of what passes for intellectual debate within the public management community.

Leadership Counts

An important vein of literature is concerned with the existential problem of the public executive as leader and with the role of leadership in achieving the aims of public policy in a political context.

New work appearing in the 1980s began to reflect the growing influence of the cases-of-practice orientation on public management scholarship. Martin Levin and Barbara Ferman (1986), for example, arguing that implementation continues to be "the knottiest aspect of policymaking," studied the implementation of nine youth employment programs authorized by the 1977 Youth Employment Demonstration Project Act (YEDPA). Their goal was "to build an impressionistic model of the conditions that contribute to effective implementation" (p. 314). Their impressions included the following: program executives used incentives and inducements to turn mild interest among potential stakeholders into active support; they used local stakeholder networks to good advantage; the programs' goals were modest, straightforward, and relatively nonthreatening to local interests; and successful executives anticipated pitfalls and fixed problems as they arose.

In "Effective Implementation and Its Limits" (1986), on the basis of his survey of implementation cases, Levin lists conditions contributing to effective implementation. The most important was "talented executives" (p. 218), though he qualifies this condition by noting that talent is idiosyncratic and hard to replicate. Other favorable conditions include "a favorable context," the assistance of "private interest groups," "a new organization," and "coercion." Levin insists that "these conclusions are not tautological in that in many circumstances *the opposite of these conclusions does hold*" (p. 227; italics in original). They are not truisms because "they focus the readers on conditions to which they otherwise would pay insufficient attention" (p. 227).

Jameson Doig and Erwin Hargrove's *Leadership and Innovation: A Biographical Perspective on Entrepreneurs in Government* (1987) is a work that falls in the gray area between public management, "traditional" public administration, and political science, influenced as it was by all three. The work is significant for at least two reasons. First, as Neustadt points out in the preface, it takes the strategic problem of turning formal authority into effective influence from the federal presidency "one and two levels down, into the executive branch, and deals with it illustratively, biographically, from person to person" (p. vii). Second, it derives a potentially important idea from its dozen empirical chapters: achievement is associated with the occurrence of a favorable match between individual skills and organizational tasks within a favorable historical/political context.

The skills are likely to be entrepreneurial (a conclusion hard to avoid, since they began with subjects who were, by any reasonable standard, entrepreneurs): "a capacity to engage in systematic rational analysis; an ability to see new possibilities offered by the evolving historical situation; and a desire to 'make a difference' " (p. 11). But possession of these skills does not guarantee success. "Almost all of our thirteen subjects experienced significant reverses.... [T]heir talents did not erode," but they encountered a poor fit between their skills, tasks they undertook, and contexts in which they worked.

I formulated a somewhat more elaborate version of this approach in evaluating the success or failure of five public managers, by no means all entrepreneurs, appointed by President Ronald Reagan (Lynn 1985). I argued that four factors interact to account for managerial success or failure: (1) the instrumental skills and (2) the "managerial personality" of the individual executive, (3) the organizational and political context, and (4) the executive's strategic idea or design for action. Among other things, I concluded that the more demanding the tasks and the more sophisticated the design needed to carry them out effectively, the greater the premium on instrumental skills and on an individual's having a personality or disposition adaptable to a complex political environment (p. 366). In other words, many factors "count"; what counts most in a given situation depends on the relative values of all factors (i.e., on a complex "fit"). Commenting on this research, Hugh Heclo (1985) argued that

> if governance results from the joint interaction of many different parts, it follows that the appropriate unit of analysis is not appointees in bureaus, or interest groups, or the presidency, or the administration's program in Congress, or the actions of the courts. The appropriate unit of analysis is the cluster of interrelated parts that produces the results by which we are governed. (p. 374)

Actor- or program-focused empirical research risked ignoring or relegating to the periphery significant, perhaps decisive, explanatory factors.

A more overt prescriptive emphasis, later to become more fashionable, is incorporated in Douglas Yates's *The Politics of Management* (1987). Concerned with both public and private organizations but richly illustrated with public examples, Yates's book is concerned to show "the centrality of bureaucratic politics and conflict management in all organizations.... [T]he effective leader [is] a skilled manager of political conflict and the effective organization [is] one that has designed ways of dealing with its own internal conflicts in productive rather than destructive ways." The end result will be that we perceive substantial imperfection in our policies, organizations, decisions, and leaders. The central problem facing would-be leaders is "how to play more than one role successfully, how to combine more than one strength, and how also to know which occasion calls for which style of leadership" (p. 242).

Drawing primarily on conceptual and empirical literature concerned with organizational and political analysis, Yates argues, in particular, that managers should create and nurture "a competitive policy debate ... an open, frankly combative dialogue in which major points of difference and conflicting interest are fought out among affected parties" in a neutral language and in a spirit of mutual respect, inclusiveness, and commitment to achieving mutual gains.

In *The Politics of Public Management* (1987), Philip Heymann seeks to distill from his own government experience as well as from "the scores of case studies of government officials' political and managerial actions" (largely ignoring academic literature in the process) insights into "the politics of management," by which he means, not bureaucratic politics in the Allison-Yates sense, but "maintaining legislative and public support of an agency and for the goals of its leader" (p. xiii). His examination concludes, drawing in particular on sixteen Kennedy School teaching cases that feature managers managing politics, that the government manager is "the helmsman of a comparatively independent organization, guided by a strategy relating it to other such organizations as well as to elected officials ... [an individual who] can sometimes even shape the very conditions of political acceptance that bound his independence...." (p. 188).

"In the final analysis," Heymann argues, "an appointed agency head's ability to direct a government organization comes from his ability to manage the politics that decides policy within the area of the organization's responsibilities" (p. 8).

> [H]andling the politics of managing a governmental agency requires choosing goals that will elicit whatever external support their execution requires because of what the goals promise to do, or what they say about who and what are important, or what alliances they invite. The goals, moreover, must be within the capacity or the attainable capacity of the organization, or else the promises and statements will prove to be empty. (p. 42)

A skeptical reader is entitled to suspect that Heymann's convictions inspired his selection of evidence, rather than the other way around.

At first glance, John DiIulio's *Governing Prisons* (1987) might appear to be too specialized to be of much interest to the general public management community. Yet his project is intriguing: determining if what sociologists call "societies of captives" can be governed in accordance with civilized standards. And his conclusion, based on detailed case studies of three state prison systems, may strike a reader as surprising: "The quality of prison life depends far more on management practices than on any other single variable.... Low levels of order, amenity, and service in prisons are neither expressions of amorphous social forces ... nor by-products of public apathy or the insensitivity of corrections officials. Poor prison conditions are produced by observable and, it appears, remediable defects in the way that prisons are organized and managed" (pp. 6, 235).

The specifics are often equally surprising. For example, DiIulio says that "bureaucratic prisons may foster higher staff morale, better inmate programs, and a more safe and civilized prison environment" (pp. 240–41) than loosely structured, noncoercive prison governments. Further, "successful prison directors and institutional managers are not here today, gone tomorrow. They are in office long enough to learn the job, make plans, and implement them. Second, they are highly 'hands on' and pro-active. They pay close attention to details and do not wait for problems to arise but attempt to anticipate them.... At the same time, they recognize the need for outside support" (p. 242). The conclusions are especially persuasive because they appear to have followed from, rather than preceded, the collection and evaluation of data.

In 1988 Behn introduced "management by groping along" into public management's conventional wisdom. "Most management concepts are simple," he argued. "And, to have any impact, these simple management ideas must be expressible in some pithy phrase" (Behn 1988, 651). Drawing on a variety of sources—case material, public officials in Massachusetts, classic teaching cases, presentations by state governors at Duke's Governors' Center, popular business literature—Behn argued that "rather than develop a detailed strategy to be followed unswervingly, a good manager establishes a specific direction—a very clear objective—and then gropes his way towards it" (p. 645).

In a "Comment" accompanying Behn's article, Alan Altshuler (1988), arguing that the public policy field is rediscovering institutions and human relationships, summarizes what he believes are the conclusions of this "rediscovery":

- Strategies are most likely to be effective when they are broad and simple, explicitly leaving tactics to be worked out in adaptive fashion as events unfold.
- The most powerful substantive strategies are typically about how to approach challenges, rather than precooked recipes for overcoming them.
- Public management at the highest levels is less about implementing precise statutes than about (a) defining agency missions within the context of broad statutory constraints, and (b) nurturing agency capabilities to carry out the missions so defined.
- The capabilities in question, notably, are as likely to be about how to stay fresh, loose, and adaptive as about how to apply techniques developed in response to past challenges.
- The best managers are not paper planners. Rather, they are restless scanners who stay closely in touch with their varied constituencies and who are constantly eager to try out (rather than formally study) new ideas. At the same time, they have a broad sense at any time of the directions in which they want to move. (p. 666).

The central (but not the only) concern of these works is the proposition that leadership counts. For some authors, its truth is assumed, and "confirming" evidence is found; for others, its truth emerges from an examination of cases. What is missing from many of these second-generation works is the meticulous concern for modeling and evidence of the early, more academic works. The balance between art and science seems to have been tipping in favor of art.

Organization Counts

A subtly contrasting vein of literature is concerned with the public executive as a more impersonal actor in a multiple-force field.

Eugene Bardach and Robert A. Kagan's *Going by the Book: The Problem of Regulatory Unreasonableness* (1982) is not, in the first instance, a book concerned with public management. The authors attempt to document the existence of a social problem, which they call regulatory unreasonableness: the tendency for programs of social regulation "to expand excessively their coverage and their stringency" or to produce too many "departures from common sense" (pp. xii, 6). The origin of regulatory unreasonableness, they argue, is the laudable desire to protect the public from discretionary acts by inspectors that might cause harm. The result is a regime of controls over the regulatory process that virtually guarantees regulatory unreasonableness: actions or nonactions that defy common sense. They reach the following important conclusion:

> The risk of having the state push accountability requirements into the farther reaches and deeper recesses of social life is that, in the long run, everyone will be accountable for everything, but no one will take responsibility for anything. Thus the social responsibility of regulators, in the end, must not simply be to impose controls, but to activate and draw upon the conscience and the talents of those they seek to regulate. (p. 323)

Thus, while the book is ostensibly about the design of regulatory arrangements, it is, at the same time, about managing the regulatory enterprise in two senses. First, in a chapter devoted to "managing the regulatory agency," Bardach and Kagan argue that though regulatory leaders are necessarily preoccupied with what Heymann calls "the politics of management," they can take steps to "encourage flexible enforcement." The authors' categories of action (incorporating many specific measures) include managing inspectors so as to increase the likelihood that discretion will be used wisely, coping rationally with resource constraints, and performing a broad educational function with respect to both regulators and the regulated. Second, an implication of their book is that, as political managers, regulatory leaders should seek to increase support for regulatory arrangements that, as they say, activate and draw on the consciences of the regulated. Thus they seek to induce managers to serve an objective derived from a close, scholarly analysis of institutional processes.

In a series of articles, Janet Weiss has pursued the notion that ideas are an instrument of public management and associates herself with "the wave of interest in generic instruments (or tools, or social technologies) for accomplishing governmental purposes" (Weiss 1990, 178). Based on an analysis of the enactment of the Community Mental Health Centers and Facilities Construction Act of 1963, she concludes that both "ideas" and "inducements" are useful to achieving the aims of public policy. She contrasts the potential power of an instruments approach with the value of emphasizing "leadership abilities": " 'leadership' is not only a conceptual morass; it also has sharply limited implications for policy. Good leaders are scarce, and cannot even be counted upon to replicate their own successes.... [T]he policy instrument perspective separates identifiable strands of activity that can be emulated across settings" (pp. 196–97).

In another article, she examined obstacles to cooperation in nine groups of local school districts. She began with the assumption that "agencies must be pushed or pulled into cooperation; they cannot be expected to embrace it naturally" (Weiss 1987, 94). She gathers information on the costs and potential gains to agencies from cooperating in addressing a shared problem. She concludes that "public managers ... cannot expect cooperation to follow from a passionate explication of [its] benefits. [They] must anticipate and manage all ... steps of the process to put into place the conditions necessary for cooperation to occur" (p. 114).

In a series of papers extending over a decade and intellectually anchored in mainstream political science, Evelyn Brodkin has developed the idea of policy politics as an administrative activity with significant consequences for the outcomes of public policy. In a 1987 article, she argues that "administrative agencies have adapted to weaknesses in the political institutions of governance, weaknesses that result in policy stalemate and disorganized political conflict. That adaptation involves the transformation of policy politics from its more contentious, democratic form into an administrative form that is more manageable" (Brodkin 1987, 585) and apparently more technical, nonpolitical, and, worse, inaccessible to citizen influence and democratic control.

Brodkin points to the implications of policy politics for public management: "the institutions that deliver social policy influence the agendas and strategies of policy entrepreneurs ... competition among institutions may preempt policy options or make them costly to policy entrepreneurs.... the efforts of public executives to press their own agendas on organizations are frequently exercises in frustration" (Brodkin 1990, 114).

In a later paper Brodkin (1992) advances two propositions concerning the relationship between what may be termed political entrepreneurship and policy politics: (1) "Problem definitions that draw attention to an issue enhance its prospects of winning a place on the crowded policy agenda, but create difficulties for policy formulation by mobilizing diverse groups with competing interests" (p. 164). (2) "Policy proposals that oversimplify problems, overstate solutions, and mask competing objectives may help promote coalition-building necessary to advance policies through the legislative process; but such policies, when enacted, create potential implementation difficulties, public dissatisfaction and even political backlash" (p. 167).

In research complementary to that of Brodkin, Jane Hannaway investigated sources of administrative growth based on carefully structured field interviews with managers in a public school system. (She labels her book-length report of this research, *Managers Managing* [1989], as an interpretative essay rather than an empirical study.) She considers two models of the growth process, an "economic model" built on the assumption that the bureaucratic manager is a rent-seeking budget maximizer, and an organizational process model, which views managers as boundedly rational and as operating within loosely coupled, rule- and process-bound bureaucratic contexts.

Hannaway concludes that "the peculiar nature of managerial work naturally encourages administrative growth" (Hannaway 1987, 122). In particular, "two constant immediate concerns of managers that promote growth, given the complex and ambiguous nature of their environments, are (1) making some sense of their world and (2) limiting their liability for negative outcomes" (p. 122). Moreover, "administrative expansion resulting from ongoing organizational processes is exceedingly hard to control" (p. 129).

In *Managing Government Operations* (1982), Stephen Rosenthal implicitly criticizes the public management field's focus on senior executives by redirecting attention away from management of glamorous issues to the "daily grind" of operations management. He applies traditional categories of operating systems—line (or flow) operations, job shops, and projects—to a wide variety of case materials in a textbook format. His aim is to familiarize students with useful schemas for thinking about governmental production. With this book, Rosenthal "attempts to fill a key gap in the literature by exploring how the responsibilities and opportunities of operations managers are shaped in predictable ways by the organizational system within which they work" (p. i). Thus it is the first book to present a fundamentally operational and technical perspective of public management.

Rosenthal draws on a deepening vein of organizational studies concerning the origins and functions of organizational structure. As many scholars will testify (e.g., Bolman and Deal 1991), top executives are apt to take an unduly narrow view of their organizations, invoking principles of "efficient organization" or "leadership" or "coordination" or the like to rationalize their attempts to deal with problems. What is needed instead is habits of mind that value critical analysis and the ability to draw on a variety of conceptual heuristics or lenses to think through issues. Rosenthal's broad conclusion is that "public officials concerned about the performance of governmental operations should try to introduce operational perspectives early in the process of policy formation, thereby anticipating potential problems" (p. 291).

Steven Kelman offers a similar perspective (though, curiously, without acknowledging Rosenthal) in his intellectually ambitious *Making Public Policy* (1987). Based on a life-cycle view of policymaking, he suggests that in proceeding from "policy idea" to "real world outcomes," "production" be used as a framework for analysis and prescription concerning achieving the aims of public policy. During production, governmental organizations create outputs. Indeed, in its emphasis on organizational functions, and its deemphasis on decision making, entrepreneurship, and the executive function, Kelman's book is, in spirit, migrating back in the direction of "traditional public administration."

Similar in its meticulous empirical work to books of some years back is Kelman's *Procurement and Public Management* (1990). Further developing a theme from his earlier book, he says that "the problem with the current system [of government procurement] is that public officials cannot use common sense and good judgment in ways that would promote better vendor performance. I believe that the system should be significantly deregulated to allow public officials greater discretion" (p. 1). He undertook an intensive analysis of how the government buys computer technology because "a study of government computer procurement sheds light on our philosophy of management of the public sector.... An answer to why the procurement system is in trouble may also tell why management of the public sector is in trouble" (p. 3).

In his concluding chapter, Kelman duly offers prescriptions for reforming procurement, but he also offers several more general insights. "Rule-boundedness in the management of the public sector fits well with goals for public management that are limited to equity, integrity, and economy. In a complex and changing world, goals that give important place to the quality of government's substantive performance are likely to require that we give public officials more discretion" (p. 90). The sad truth, he says, is that "simply to display common sense, such as by favoring a vendor because he is good, is to court questioning, disgrace, or even prison. Unfortunately, this is the pattern for far too much of the public sector" (p. 105).

Kelman is perhaps the first public management scholar since Allison (especially in the latter's *Remaking Foreign Policy: The Organizational Connection,* written with Peter Szanton in 1976) to insist on giving priority to the proposition that structures matter to managerial and organizational performance. His analysis of case material leads him, along with Elmore, Bardach, and Kagan, to advocate deregulation of bureaucracy. Elsewhere, Kelman has argued that citizens should

> judge organizations by results, not by whether they have followed bureaucratic rules.... [T]he excessive reliance on rules involves an intellectual failure to understand that the fear of discretion extracts a high price in terms of poor substantive government performance.... A part of the battle against the fear of discretion in gov-

ernment management must be waged in the realm of ideas. (Kelman 1991, 196)

In contrast to much of the "leadership counts" literature, these works address more complex questions: How and under what circumstances does leadership count? How do mandates, organizations, and institutional arrangements shape leader behavior? Toward what institutional goals ought leaders direct their efforts? Many of these works are, as well, more scholarly in the traditional academic sense, perhaps because many of their authors are in academic settings with closer ties to the social science community.

Public Management as Homiletics

In 1982, Thomas J. Peters and Robert H. Waterman, Jr., published *In Search of Excellence: Lessons from America's Best-Run Companies*. Part of an emerging stream of consulting firm scholarship, the book began with a scathing attack on "the rational model," a legacy of Frederick Taylor that was leading managers astray. The authors deplored numeralist, rationalist management based on "detached, analytical justification" (p. 29), with its built in conservative bias that ignored "the messy human stuff." They celebrated managers who acquired "a gut feeling for the gestalt of their businesses" and identified and illustrated with examples eight attributes of "the best-run companies" (pp. 13–16), including "a bias for action," "close to the customer," and "autonomy and entrepreneurship."

The mockery of rationalism, the epistemology of "common sense," and the celebration of "successful managers" with distinct, assertive voices were to be widely emulated in the literature of public management. Its success was, and is, an inspiration to teachers of public management who sought to inspire and empower public executives. Anxious to inspire public officials with the conviction that "management counts" and an entrepreneurial, proactive spirit, the public policy schools turned heavily to prescription.

Behn's *Leadership Counts* (1991) is a didactic, even tendentious, book. Based on his study of how a team of policy entrepreneurs pursued welfare reform in the Commonwealth of Massachusetts, Behn takes on prevailing "myths": policy determines action, administration is control, and competent management is businesslike. He advocates, instead, the "Leadership Metastrategy ... the cornerstone of which is an inspiring mission combined with a specific goal" (p. 203). Indeed, the essence of public management is tireless advocacy of the mission and the goals. As for the means, "the field will figure out how to do it" (p. 204), and a good manager will empower employees to figure things out.

In the end, Behn cautions, the matter is not so simple. "For success—for results—the manager must put together policy, administration, and leadership" (p. 206). But the emphasis must be on that "under-utilized strategy": leadership. Without it, I take Behn to be saying, solving specific administrative problems—coordination, motivation, technique, budgets, overhead agencies, politics—will become ends in themselves and produce the organizational pathologies (a preoccupation with serving the organization's needs instead of producing results) that public management's leaders ought to be seeking to overcome.

Reich's equally didactic but less tendentious *Public Management in a Democratic Society* (1990) is a casebook of eleven cases, some hoary veterans of public management classrooms. Most are "decision- forcing," ending just at the point where the public manager has to take action. Says Reich in introducing the material, "I then ask you to imagine that you are the manager and must decide what to do." To each case is appended a kind of teaching note that concludes with lessons that reflect Reich's themes.

Reich's central theme is achieving "effective and responsive public management," a problem he labels a dilemma. Emphasizing effectiveness through manipulation and subversion of politics turns you into Robert Moses. Emphasizing responsiveness renders you passive, an agent of biased and incoherent results. The way out of this dilemma is to foster "deliberation," ongoing, give-and-take conversation that establishes goals and expectations, thereby facilitating a manager's own accountability. His concluding sentence is this: "Properly understood, politics and law and not constraints on effective public action; they are sources of knowledge and wisdom about public purposes" (p. 105).

Michael Barzelay's *Breaking Through Bureaucracy: A New Vision for Managing in Government* (1992) advances the argument that public management cultures must be transformed by infusing them with the spirit that has inspired recent corporate management reforms: motivating employee commitment, tapping employee knowledge, and unleashing employee ingenuity. He sees this type of reform as a successor to earlier waves of administrative reform: (1) civil service protection, the short ballot, state government reorganization, executive budgeting, and competitive purchasing (p. 215 n. 14); (2) program budgeting, program evaluation, and policy analysis (p. 213 n. 1); and now, (3) customers, quality, service, value, incentives, innovation, empowerment, and flexibility (p. 115).[4]

Under the sponsorship of the Program on Innovations in State and Local Government, a joint venture of the Ford Foundation and Kennedy School, Barzelay undertook a detailed study of Minnesota's "Striving toward Excellence in Performance (STEP)" program, an innovation award winner, as an exemplary case study of an effort to transform staff/line/overseer relations on behalf of better service to Minnesota citizens. In conducting his research, Barzelay collaborated extensively with the leaders of that effort, and one of them has been a collaborator. Altshuler's introduction to the book says that Barzelay's approach is "to learn from pathbreaking practice, all the while considering how it might fare in other settings" (p. xi).

Barzelay's intellectual aim is to create a "post-bureaucratic paradigm" that builds on prior practical and intellectual work. To high-

---

4. Those who view a customer orientation as a postbureaucratic discovery might ponder the following remarkable quote from a 1936 publication by a "traditional" public administrationist, Marshall Dimock: "The customer-satisfaction criterion applies with as much force to government as to business. In the past the failure of public enterprises generally to pay sufficient attention to customer attitudes and citizen relations has been the aspect of public administration which is most inefficient and open to criticism. . . . If the administrator keeps his eyes constantly on the end result, namely customer satisfaction, then the steps which need to be taken in order to improve the internal administration are usually self-apparent" (Dimock 1936, 126).

light issues, he sets up an ingenious (though not wholly ingenuous) hypothetical dialogue among Defender (of the status quo), Social Scientist (who explains, and, therefore, implicitly legitimizes the status quo),[5] and Progressive Thinker (who would transform the status quo in the name of higher values). The deus ex machina is "Possibilist," who is convinced that staff/line/overseer problems are common but eminently solvable and who finds all three prior positions wanting. To make his case, Possibilist turns to Minnesota's STEP program for an example of what he means.

To Possibilist, the problem must be conceived as one of "accountability." Barzelay suggests the rhetorical standard: "results citizens value" (p. 119). To establish or redirect accountability, a variety of strategies—classified as changes in constraints, incentives, and routines—is available. Once accomplished, these changes, with their rhetorical justifications, constitute a change in the organization's culture. The justifications, which take the form of "principles" legitimized through "deliberation" within the organization, constitute the postbureaucratic paradigm. Examples of such principles include "Spread Responsibility for Economizing and Compliance"; "Conceptualize Work as Providing Services"; "Identify Customers with Care"; "Be Accountable to Customers"; "Reorganize to Separate Service from Control"; "Let the Customers Fund the Providers." In a summary paragraph, Barzelay lists the emerging managerial virtues:

> The post-bureaucratic paradigm values argumentation and deliberation about how the roles of public managers should be framed. Informed public managers today understand and appreciate such varied role concepts as exercising leadership, creating an uplifting mission and organizational culture, strategic planning, managing without direct authority, pathfinding, problem setting, identifying customers, groping along, reflecting-in-action, coaching, structuring

---

5. Social Scientist is evidently unacquainted with a variety of literatures, primarily in journals, on institutions and incentives, for example, transaction costs and their implications, problems of agency, collective action problems inside organizations, and the like.

incentives, championing products, instilling a commitment to quality, creating a climate for innovation, building teams, redesigning work, investing in people, negotiating mandates, and managing by walking around. (p. 132)

Despite claims to the contrary, *Breaking Through Bureaucracy* seems to be firmly, and ironically, within two traditions commonly associated with traditional public administration: dichotomizing politics and administration, because political processes as a source of legitimacy are left out of Barzelay's analysis; and looking to the business sector for principles that can be applied to government, because the product/customer focus slights the fact that the source of public revenues, especially for collective goods, is neither customers nor the sale of products. These predispositions are particularly evident in the section on "From Justifying Costs to Delivering Value" (pp. 130–31), which simply ignores budgetary politics and its influence on governmental processes. It is also evident in the sources cited by Barzelay, which are largely drawn from the business literature (p. 181 n. 25). Bureaucracies, then, are viewed, much as Max Weber viewed them, as self-willed entities that may (and should) seek to be accountable to citizens but that are beyond the influence of the mechanisms of social choice.

In *Making Government Work: How Entrepreneurial Executives Turn Bright Ideas into Real Results* (1994), Martin Levin and Mary Bryna Sanger set out to demonstrate through numerous examples that "management matters," that management is vital to policy success. In a book that is "about real life, not theoretical principles," they emulate the by-now familiar Peters and Waterman style: successful bureaucratic entrepreneurs are action-oriented, turn seemingly insurmountable obstacles into opportunities, trust learning by doing, act without a complete plan and risk making mistakes. "There is more to fear from paralysis of analysis than from action" (p. 313). Vision. Moving forward rapidly. Vigilance. "This is a far cry from the public policy schools' recommendation that public managers use policy analysis" (p. 314). To the contrary, "public management is about values."

A kind of pinnacle of the prescriptive literature was scaled by

Richard N. Haass, who, like Gordon Chase and Robert Reich, is an experienced public official who taught at the Kennedy School of Government. His *The Power to Persuade* (1994) is subtitled *How to Be Effective in Government, the Public Sector, or Any Unruly Organization*. Testimonials on the book's dust jacket are provided by Tom Peters, Richard Neustadt, former U.S. Senator Howard Baker, former President of the Urban League and Clinton adviser Vernon Jordan, and, with the ultimate accolade, Ted Koppel of the television production "Nightline."

The Power to Persuade is advertised as "the only book to tell managers in government and other public sector organizations how to improve performance when there is no clear bottom line." It is all tough, no-nonsense talk (e.g., "Don't break the law"). It is studded with lists of guidelines and principles. To exert influence, asks Haass, "What Does It Take?" The answer is, follow "The Five Principles," which are these:

- Develop and focus on a narrow agenda.
- Look for opportunities to act.
- Bring honesty and integrity to all that you do.
- Be careful.
- Pay attention to people.

"Being effective is that simple—and that complicated," concludes Haass. There is a role for mental activity in Haass's world. In order to "be careful," you must, among other things, "be careful with facts, mindful of assumptions, rigorous in your analysis" (p. 230). Nevertheless, care in this sense is given no more weight than watching what you say.

Thus many scholars and teachers have assumed away all but the most idiosyncratic, psychological aspects of managerial roles, leading to a highly reductive view of public management. Public managers have been reduced to mock heroic figures. Research has been reduced to culling examples of whatever the author seeks to celebrate from the countless instances of things happening in the world.

The heroic takes two forms. In the first form, successful managers have acquired a generic psychological state, perhaps determined largely by personality. Thus successful managers may be characterized as enterprising or entrepreneurial, disposed to take risks, purposeful, imaginative and intuitive, inclined to act. In the second form, successful managers follow a generic process that is experientially justified and not explicitly or even necessarily analytical. Thus successful managers establish goals and hold subordinates to their achievement, then walk around to clarify, inspire, and monitor. Rejecting effete, conservative rationalism, these reductive authors have little praise for the manager who is contemplative, analytical, intellectually curious or clever, problem driven, or knowledgeable.

Richard P. Nathan is an exemplar of the antianalytical reductionist school. In a letter to an incoming public executive, Nathan (1993, 139; italics added) would say: "You asked me to recommend books on management. I like the Peters and Waterman book *In Search of Excellence* .... They are skeptical of fancy analysis, the rational actor model, and elaborate planning. Their needling about business schools is right on, for example where they talk about 'paralysis by analysis.' ... [M]anagement at the top in both business and government is an art form. *It is a function of style and situation.*"

What's New?

When members of the public administration community and the public policy community refer to public management, they are not speaking the same language, or are they pursuing the same intellectual agenda.

The leaders of the effort to create a new field of public policy analysis proclaimed a decisive break with traditional public administration. Public policy's public management community has shown little subsequent inclination toward comity with its sister province in public administration. There was then and is now a rather patronizing "attitude" toward public administration within the public policy community.[6]

In reaction to the claim to ownership of the term and the sub-

6. For a recent expression, see John J. DiIulio, Jr. (1990, 117).

ject by members of the public policy community, public administrationists are apt to be defensive. Donald F. Kettl (1990, 411–12), for example, cites challenges to public administration from three directions, implementation, public management, and rational choice, which have "wounded its self-confidence and its self-awareness." Kettl sees public management as the case- and practitioner-based emphasis on top administrative leaders and how they engage in the strategic management of programs and the securing and maintenance of political support. While "useful," in their exclusive focus on the agency's top levels, the public management school (public policy's version, not public administration's)

> blinds itself to important questions.... The public-management school gives few clues about how to deal with other [than top] levels of the bureaucracy, or how those levels behave (except, perhaps, as an impediment to executive action). The public-management school thus gives few clues about how administration works—and why it sometimes does not. (pp. 413, 414)

To a public administrationist, then, a typical public manager is, first and foremost, a practicing professional within the field of public administration, not a political appointee with other primary societal affiliations (Perry and Kraemer 1983). The "unit of analysis" is the governmental organization, not the policy, program, social problem, or incumbent of an executive position. The "essential readings" compiled by Ott, Hyde, and Shafritz (1991) and a parallel volume compiled by the principal authors in the preceding section would, I am certain, have virtually no readings in common.

Two apparent ironies are worth noting. One is that, within public administration, public management is commonly regarded as less "normative" than traditional public administration, more instrumental or technocratic. Within the public policy community, in contrast, public management is, or is becoming, more "normative" than traditional public policy analysis, less scientific and disinterested. Within the public administration community, public management, it seems, cools the passions; within the public policy community, it inflames them.

A second irony, identified by Alasdair Roberts (1995), is more subtle but more significant. By taking a homiletic turn toward the promotion of "civic discovery" as the norm for public managers, public management experts such as Moore and Reich are reinventing an old wheel: the politics-administration dichotomy. A process of civic discovery, Roberts argues, necessarily requires impartiality by public managers if citizens are to trust the process as essentially fair. Thus is reified the venerable concept of neutral competence long associated with the view that politics and administration are governed by separate procedural and normative logics. Thus do the advocates for recovery and renewal within the public administration and the proponents of civic discovery within the public policy community become soulmates.

Caught in an eddy off this strong mainstream current toward homiletics is the issue with which public management's scholars were once preoccupied: achieving the balance of art and science that would place the performance of the public executive role on new and stronger intellectual foundations. Is the field moving in the right direction in abandoning its aspirations to achieve such a balance?

4

STATECRAFT
AND SKILL

[A] government ill executed, whatever it may be in theory, must
be, in practice, a bad government.

— Alexander Hamilton

W|hatever else may be included in its scope, public manage-
ment is essentially concerned with the performance of
the executive function in government. This function is
divided among numerous actors, none of whom exercises the whole
of it. Public management necessarily takes place within a larger domain of policies, institutions, and actors. The vantage point of any
particular actor is necessarily incomplete, the range of influence limited. For the practitioner, contending with the centrifugal forces of
political life can be disorienting. For the scholar and teacher, distinguishing figure and ground may prove difficult.

A strategic tension pervades the executive function, moreover.
This tension can be usefully, if somewhat simplistically, understood
as one between Jeffersonian and Hamiltonian concepts of governance. Shall the emphasis in public management be on obtaining popular and stakeholder guidance before the fact, that is, on political
consultation and public deliberation as the sources of legitimacy for
executive purposes? Or shall the emphasis be on producing results

and being judged by them, that is, on after-the-fact accountability, on performance and evaluation within the constraints of public law?

Apart from their philosophical and programmatic implications, these two emphases require different kinds of executives. Jeffersonian management requires skill in consultation, negotiation, and communication, the skillful probing for public understanding and consent (Yates 1982; Reich 1990; Lindblom 1990; Schon and Rein 1994). Hamiltonian management requires a skilled decision maker, organizer, and "executive" in the literal sense: one suited for formulating and carrying out plans and duties. Therefore, a choice of emphasis has an important bearing on public management research, teaching, and practice.

Some may argue that the two notions of governance are not mutually exclusive, that they can and must be reconciled (Reich 1990; Levin and Sanger 1994). This is the view, for example, of Robert Reich, who refers to the tension I have described as the "effectiveness-responsiveness dilemma."

Arguing against choosing either emphasis (albeit following the Peters and Waterman precedent, in caricatured form), Reich advocates an approach he terms "deliberative." As a public manager, you propose, you listen, you adjust; you are simultaneously proactive and reactive, sponsoring ideas and probing the ideas of others until action is warranted.

This is a useful rhetorical device, but it and similar devices such as "probing" (Lindblom 1990) and "frame reflection" (Schon and Rein 1994) fail, I think, as constituting guidance for creating and communicating "knowledge for practice."

Public managers face specific demands in particular contexts. While deliberation may describe an appropriate temperamental orientation, it cannot be a generic solution to specific problems. A manager's choice of process may lead to convergence or divergence, consent or dissent, focus or confusion, endorsement of the status quo or its rejection. Solutions require reflection and analysis and specific designs that address basic contextual matters. The issues for scholars and teachers concern the subjects for deliberation and when, how, and with whom these deliberations should be conducted if they are to stimulate rather than stifle action.

Choice and Execution

At the heart of public management, whether Jeffersonian or Hamiltonian, is a strategic judgment: a choice concerning goals and actions in specific settings that satisfies reasonable criteria. Following Heclo (1977), I shall term the continuing exercise of such executive judgment "statecraft." The statecraft of political administration, Heclo argues, is "office-using by people in a variety of circumstances at the top of the executive branch" (p. 3) or, more specifically, "how political leaders choose to act" (p. 155). The real test of a political executive's statecraft "is his ability to institute the changes he wants without losing the bureaucratic services he requires" (p. 181).

"Governmental performance," Heclo argues further, "can be thought of as the product of political leadership times bureaucratic power." By political leadership, he refers to the tasks of direction-setting and heat-taking: "the craft of using and risking [democratic political] power through action" (p. 7). Political executives move in two worlds: "the tight, ingrown village life of the bureaucratic community and the open, disjointed world of political strangers" (p. 112). Success means "moving government actions in some intended direction" (p. 155). Unlike presidential or gubernatorial politics, where electoral outcomes are at stake, bureaucratic politics "contemplates quiet, behind-the-scenes workmanship, strategic reversals, caution, contentment with results for which everyone can share some of the credit" (p. 223). And, Heclo argues, executives and, in particular, how executives choose to conduct themselves, are important. We will never have management without managers, Heclo insists. "No reforms are likely to change the basic need for statecraft in political administration" (p. 249).

There can be little doubt, then, that effective public management requires the consistent exercise of good judgment under the most demanding and disorienting circumstances. Thus the effective practice of public management requires individuals with extraordinary attributes. The arguable issue is the nature of these attributes. What are the roots of statecraft?

Unfortunately, the sizable literature concerned with managerial success has produced few, if any, robust insights concerning effectiveness. In the field of "leadership studies," for example, investigators are apt to find what they are looking for, and every kind of explanation has been looked for and found. Some investigators emphasize a manager's goals or sense of direction or values as essential to success. A related view stresses a manager's strength of character or stability and wholesomeness of personality, the ability to arouse and inspire by moral and ethical example. Other investigators call attention to core managerial skills: competence in grasping problems, performing tasks, making decisions, and motivating and organizing work. Still others stress a manager's political acumen, the ability to find common ground among opponents, and skill in political tactics and managing across boundaries. All such views have merit; none, it seems safe to say, is sufficient by itself.

Perhaps the most resonant truth emerging from the study of effectiveness is that success is apt to reflect a good fit between individual capabilities and the demands of specific situations (Doig and Hargrove 1987). Individuals of widely varying skills and attributes can be effective depending on the circumstances. The proper study of public management in this view involves the study of good fits between people and circumstances. Yet the matter is not so easily settled. There are the vital questions of the different contexts within which public executives work, differences among executives themselves, and, of particular importance, the content of the interactions between executives and their circumstances (Wilson 1989). What, exactly, is a good fit? Unfortunately, the prospects for good fits may not be transparent a priori, and they may not be replicable ex post.

The key question for scholars and teachers of public management in professional schools is what, if anything, public executives can do to make a given fit work. Statecraft as choice and execution from an exposed position implies executive ability, based on knowledge, experience, and aptitudes, to choose deliberately and with care and to do the chosen thing well. These would seem to be skills that can be learned, and the question is how they can be identified and taught.

Not everyone who has studied complex organizations agrees that learned skills, most particularly analytical skills, are essential to making the most of one's circumstances. Charles Lindblom, for example, has identified three kinds of successful practices: technologies, for which good practice can be systematically described and therefore taught; crafts, or skilled activities that cannot be completely reduced to a code of prescriptions but for which skill can be enhanced through demonstration and apprenticeship; and indeterminate practices, for which success cannot be accounted for a priori (Lindblom 1981, 246). "Good decision-making in organizations," Lindblom believes, "is an indeterminate practice." So, many will argue (a fortiori, some would add), is public management, encompassing as it does numerous, far less articulated activities than decision making.

One's judgment in the issue raised by Lindblom has, as my earlier discussion implied, important programmatic implications for the field. Preparing for a technocratic practice involves acquiring codified knowledge that is relatively straightforward, if not easy, to describe and mastering demonstrable, replicable skills together with a body of techniques for their application. Preparing for an indeterminate practice is an altogether less straightforward matter, involving lengthy socialization and acculturation and subtle forms of nearly aesthetic mastery: the ability to create and sustain vision for an agency, to lead by example, to insinuate oneself into a social reality and a historical process.

Review of public management's rhetorical literature might suggest that this question—technology, craft, or indeterminate practice—already has a consensus answer. Few would label public management a technology. Few would go as far as Lindblom presumably would in the opposite direction and label public management an indeterminate practice. Most scholars and teachers of public management have become comfortable with the term craft, in the sense that, as Majone puts it, "successful performance depends on an intimate knowledge of materials, tools, and processes, and on a highly personal relationship between agent and task" (Majone 1980, 9). Indeed, the term craft is frequently applied (e.g., by Majone) to the most technocratic of public policy's subfields: policy analysis. Good practice, whether of formal policy analysis or of public management, is a balance of know-how and feel.

Declaring public management a craft in general and statecraft in particular might appear to settle most questions concerning the direction that ought to be taken by the field's scholars and teachers if they are to contribute to successful practice. Unfortunately, we are still not at the point where research, curriculums, and practice strategies can be mapped out.

Awaiting the Millennium

Addressing the question as to what political science can contribute to the study of public management and the improvement of practitioner skill, David Weimer exposes perhaps the most fundamental issue of public management content, albeit inadvertently:

> Political science might contribute to the improvement of practitioner skill by more explicitly considering ... the rules and incentives that constrain and motivate practice.... But students of public management who focus their attention on managers as decision makers seem to be asking a different question: What can political science contribute to the improvement of practitioner skill, *taking institutional arrangements as given?* An overview of the major intellectual approaches within political science suggests the answer is "not much." (1992b, 241–42; italics added)

This highly consequential assumption—that institutional arrangements are given, that management is a series of short runs—perhaps originated with Joseph Bower's trenchant observation that "the United States has very nearly denied the public executive the tools of management. It is almost true that the business executive's enabling resources—structure and people—are the public executive's constraints" (Bower 1977). This view has become popular in the public policy community. (The public administration community seems to reject such a restrictive view, although most treatments of administrative practice depict the administrator's role as custodian rather than designer of institutions.) Behn argues that "any emphasis on the perspective of practicing public managers will have a short-run focus."[1] Levin (1986) is more expansive:

1. Robert D. Behn, personal correspondence with the author, 28 April 1993.

Some observers have argued for the need to alter political and institutional structure in order to create the conditions for innovation. But while *awaiting this millennium,* our research suggests that even within these constraints, there is a good deal that managers can do to improve their organizations. We focus on what entrepreneurial managers have done *within the existing organizational environment.* (p. 270; italics added)

Restricting public management's intellectual agenda to, as Moore put it, "realiz[ing] the potential of a given political and institutional setting," has unfortunate intellectual and practical consequences. Questions concerning the manager's role in the design of political institutions and the long-run performance of organizations, and interest in the disciplines that address such institutional/organizational questions, will necessarily be deemphasized. Attention will be directed instead to identifying those actions and psychological states that are conducive to achieving immediate payoffs, where one must live by one's wits, not by one's grasp of deeper structures.[2] Effective public management is for the most part—though no one would put it this way—ephemeral.

This short-run focus would not be altogether fatal to intellectual depth if "given contexts" were modeled to show how variance in constraints across settings affects how managers go about realizing their potential and with what consequences. (For examples, see Lynn 1985; Lynn and Smith 1982.) But modeling usually means imposing a priori notions on data collection, multiple case research, and rigorous analysis, disciplines no longer in favor with scholars and teachers oriented to the here and now. Behn readily concedes that "there is a methodological bias; it is much easier to identify short-run payoffs . . . than it is to identify . . . long-run payoffs."[3]

There is a more fundamental criticism lurking in the background of this debate: the hostility to the rational choice paradigm assumed to be synonymous with the term "analytical" in policy

2. The most useful intellectual formulation of such a bounded approach to management remains Herbert Simon (1964).
3. See note 1.

studies. Though popularized by Peters and Waterman, a scholarly version of this hostility made, for example, by advocates of "postpositivist" social science, is that instrumental rationality in policy analysis, with its emphasis on prediction and control, is profoundly antidemocratic (Fischer 1993). Thus it is not only "exceptional common sense" (Peters and Waterman 1982, xiii) but deeply Jeffersonian/Madisonian idealism that justifies an antirationalist stance.

The debate is not so polarized as all that, however. Two recent studies suggest a revival of interest in institutions. Barzelay argues that

> Public Management scholarship modulates and extends several traditions of thinking and writing about public affairs, public organizations, professions, and individual action. The traditions include public administration, planning, public policy implementation, and administrative law. The modulations and extensions include developing the concept of organizational strategy in the public sector; addressing directly and systematically the role of unelected officials in the policymaking process; adapting conceptions of public administration to a context of organizational, social, and technological complexity; and studying the functions and practice of leadership in the public domain (1992, p.1).

Thus Barzelay sees public management as broader than immediate gratification of political ambition, including "conceptions of public administration." From a different perspective, Kelman sees the mission of professional schools as contributing to "the growth of a public management professional culture" that values the *production of public services* (1987, 281; italics added).[4]

4. In this, he is echoing Rosenthal, who, in *Managing Government Operations* (1982), implicitly criticizes public management's focus on senior executives by redirecting attention away from glamorous issues to the "daily grind" of operations management. Rosenthal applies traditional categories of operating systems—line (or flow) operations, job shops, and projects—to specific cases, concluding that "public officials concerned about the performance of governmental operations should try to intro-

As metaphors, "production" and "operations" direct attention to structural issues and are more likely to lead to an appreciation of the sciences of organizations and institutions, and to the larger forces shaping executive effectiveness, than metaphors such as leadership, entrepreneurship, or innovation, which cast public executives in heroic, erumpent poses succeeding in spite of the system. The latter are in favor, however, with implications that are likely to be unfortunate for managerial effectiveness. If statecraft is restricted to what can be done here and how, and only by entrepreneurial risk takers, then the scope for effective practice shrinks to little more than symbolic acts.

Technique or Vision?

There are issues other than the malleability of institutions, however, that affect strategies for research, teaching, and practice. How should craftsmanship be defined and taught? Some would emphasize "knowledge of materials, tools, and processes" (i.e., a Hamiltonian emphasis), while others would emphasize "personal relationship between agent and task" (i.e., a Jeffersonian emphasis). Disagreements take two forms: that between experience or heuristics, and that between principles or rules.

Experience or Heuristics?

One argument is between advocates of knowledge distilled from field experience into generally applicable principles—an approach that has come to be known as the "best practice" school—on the one hand, and knowledge based on the empirical validation of useful propositions derived from a priori models—what I term the "applied heuristics" school—on the other. Chester Barnard (1968) is the model for best practice research (see his preface to *The Functions of the Executive*, which advocates practice as the basis for scholarship,

---

duce operational perspectives early in the process of policy formation, thereby anticipating potential problems" (1982, 291).

rather than the other way around). Simon, Thompson, and Smith-burg (1991) and, in general, the Carnegie School (as exemplified, for example, by Allison's *Essence of Decision* (1971, 20ff), is the model for building practice wisdom on a conceptually grounded, reality-tested knowledge base.

The best practice approach is fundamentally experiential. Donald A. Schon's "reflective practitioner" (1983) might appear to capture the essence of this kind of managerial practice. Abandon the seductive notion, conventionally associated with professionalism, that success in practice requires technical rationality, he advises, in favor of "reflection in action," a constant interaction between manager and context in which both may be altered in the process.

Following Schon, Lee Bolman and Terrence Deal (1991) advocate artistry as the basis for managerial effectiveness: interpreting experience and expressing it in a form that can be felt, understood, and appreciated by others. Bolman and Deal are more pragmatic about it, however: artistry is not a replacement for or alternative to technology but an essential enhancement of it. Artistry allows for the emotion, subtlety, and ambiguity surrounding issues that might nonetheless have a technical core. Whatever an individual's technical skills, "the leader as artist will rely on images as well as memos, poetry as well as policy, reflection as well as command, and reframing as well as refitting" (p. 19).

In a recent book (1994), Schon, with co-author Martin Rein, put forward the concept of "frame reflection" as a process for dealing with the complex policy issues that dominate what they call "policy practice," which includes public management. Urging rejection of reliance on analysis governed by normal social science protocols, they advise scholars and teachers to collaborate with practitioners toward the goal of understanding the bases for practitioner thought and action.[5] Scholars thus deployed will contribute to the collaboration a concern for identifying an adequate causal logic for

5. If used with managers, frame reflection would constitute a "hermeneutics" of public management, a form of the *Geisteswissenschaften* in which the goal of study is discovery of the meanings that managerial reality holds for practitioners. For an overview of social science methods that

the circumstances in question. On the basis of this understanding, scholars and teachers may be in a position to assist practitioners actively to reflect on the "frames" or mindsets that motivate their behavior and, perhaps, to change those frames that are inimical to policy success.

Taken literally, such views might appear to doom systematic research based on "normal" social science ideas as well as pre-professional education featuring analytic practice. Even if managerial success cannot be accounted for a priori, however, the odds for success can be increased by exposing as many actual or potential managers as possible, through vicarious experience in studying cases and through supervised workshops and internships, to the practice of self-conscious reflection leading toward identifying the causal logic of actual policy and management problems. As Schon and Rein recognize, conceptual models from the social sciences might well prove helpful in such inquiry. Out of such reflection will come insights that, though varying among individuals and contexts, will nonetheless improve the prospects for effective behavior by inculcating open-mindedness, an instinct for alert observation, respect for details, an instinct for causal ordering, and a proactive orientation.

The necessary intimacy for best practice can be attained, then, through the tutoring of actual or vicarious exposure to, as Peters and Waterman would put it, the gestalt of management. Scholarship would be concerned with sorting and classifying these tasks in useful ways and identifying behaviors that, *ex post,* have, in particular hands, proven effective. From such activity there will emerge *ex ante* principles, frames, stories, and checklists to compose a repertoire of stencils or "moves" for effective managerial behavior or best practice.

Best practice scholars doubt that, compared to practice wisdom distilled inductively (and intuitively) from cases and episodes of managerial activity, conventional theory-driven social science has much beyond the trivial to offer those who seek intimate knowledge

---

is relevant to the argument in this monograph, see Lindblom (1990, 135–56).

of public management's materials, tools, and processes. Most academics of the best practice persuasion seem convinced by Dror's view that "policymaking [is] an existential phenomenon … much too complex and dynamic to be fully caught in concepts, models, and theories" (Dror 1983, x).[6]

If, in contrast to this experientialist view, one believes that intellectual materials, tools and processes are essential elements of management, then a different, more analytic approach to research and teaching is required.

An analytic approach begins with the assumption that public managers confront "a messy reality" of data, observations, opinions, facts, and, not to be missed, human beings. A manager's intellectual task is to understand or explain messy reality toward the goal of gaining sufficient control over events to influence the future intentionally, for example, secure the adoption of a policy, see to the implementation of that policy with a minimum of unintended consequences, accomplish a particular result. The question is, How can this kind of instrumental understanding be achieved?

The mastery being sought is the ability to use a repertoire of analytic models as heuristics, that is, as instruments for experimenting, in a trial-and-error way, with different hypothetical approaches to complex issues and problems, whether they concern the content of and rationale for policies or the institutional and procedural means of accomplishing intended results. "Applied heuristics" was the essential method employed in the first scholarly works of public policy scholars summarized in chapter 3.

A useful elaboration of this type of social science explanation was put forth by Bendor and Hammond (1989) in the context of appraising the intellectual contributions of *Essence of Decision*. A heuristic, in their view, is one of a species of verbal, nondeductive "explanatory sketches" or conceptual frameworks that may be employed to "discover adequate explanations for puzzling phenomena"

6. In this spirit, O'Toole's evaluation of rational choice models as a basis for practice in interorganizational networks is typical: "actual implementation networks contain complications that modelling can appropriately neither ignore nor address" (1993, 15).

(p. 48). A useful heuristic has two important characteristics: (1) it yields disconfirmable propositions and is not merely "a filing system for every possible event" (Bendor 1994, 37); and (2) when applied to particular situations, it will lead reasonably often to insights that will enhance a manager's effectiveness.[7]

An example is the heuristic proposition that an agency's internal organization affects an executive's decision agenda; a functional organization will require executives to coordinate their efforts, whereas a program organization will require executives to resolve resource allocation conflicts. Applying this heuristic in a given situation may lead an executive to the insight that existing routines inappropriately restrict an executive's discretion; if internal structures are changed in particular ways, an executive's influence over agency action will probably be enhanced. If experience suggests that this heuristic, and a particular causal logic, "works" in a significant number of actual cases, that is, leads to executive reorganizations that ultimately enhance organizational performance or policy achievement, a teacher may want to include it in a public management curriculum.

From this perspective, graduate programs in public policy and administration should concentrate on assisting students to acquire skill in identifying and applying useful heuristics, thus preparing them intellectually for identifying, learning about, and solving social problems amenable to policy interventions: the issues that appear on decision agendas in political life. With some training in heuristics, supplemented by exposure to reflective practitioners, students/graduates/practitioners will be suitably prepared for apprenticeship as interns and in entry-level jobs. But schools should not attempt to teach, or at least not to emphasize, what cannot be taught—the subtle blending of policy and poetry that specific contexts require —or to waste scarce resources simulating real-world apprenticeships when the real world will do it better. Preparation for learning on the job, rather than poor simulations of the job itself, is the proper mission of professional education.

---

7. The word *heuristic,* like the word *rhetoric,* is often used inaccurately in a pejorative sense. I did so myself in Lynn (1987b) and regret it.

Principles or Rules?

Another argument concerning how to approach research and teaching, arising within the public policy community, concerns the choice between principles and rules. The end result of pursuing craft knowledge, Bardach says, may be what he calls "meaningful principles," that is, "weak but unexceptionable generalizations about what is worth attention and how a manager should prepare *psychologically* to engage with the world." The problem with statements that are "universal, timeless, deep, powerful ... [and] *never inapplicable*" is that they are not always important in prescribing for, or explaining, specific situations" (Bardach 1987, 191; italics added).

This observation has important implications for scholarship. Bardach goes on to say that "scholars can compile, clarify, and explicate ... principles; but because principles furnish meaning rather than truth, efforts at empirical validation are generally beside the point" (p. 197). It may be more useful, Bardach argues, to formulate rules: if-then statements that posit the contingent existence of a generally best way in particular situations.[8] Frederick Mayer extends this point: "We have to know whether [prescriptions] have tended to work in similar situations in the past.... If there are no similar situations [or if we cannot define them], if there is no way to generalize from experience ... , then scholars have little to say to practitioners" (1992, 323).

The universality of principles is precisely the point, argue Behn and others who see psychological preparation and the discovery of meaning as central to managerial success. Behn concedes that "the principles of management are often contradictory" (1988, 660) and "[they] can never be tested" (1992, 318). He agrees, moreover, that "all of the management principles are correct." The manager's task is "to determine which ones are relevant and how they can be adapted to the problem at hand" (1988, 660). Making such determinations is a skill most readily enhanced not by the quest for empir-

8. "Scientific energy is best spent," moreover, on improving a particular kind of rule: those "that help to protect against failure rather than those that help to effect success" (Bardach 1987, 198). In this he echoes his colleague Martin Landau (1973).

ical validation but by studying best practice just as ambitious chess students study the moves of grand masters.[9]

It is worth noting that Woodrow Wilson inaugurated the quest for "stable principle" to govern managerial behavior. Frederick Taylor and Luther Gulick brought the identification of principles to high prominence in public administration. Contemptuously labeled "proverbs" by Robert Dahl (1947) and Herbert Simon (1946), who demonstrated the mutual inconsistencies of popular principles, the appeal of principles waned. While conceding the logic of Simon's attack, however, Leonard White argued that the fact that principles are often contradictory "means only that we have not pushed our analysis far enough, or described the particular situations where one prevails rather than the other, or found criteria for weighing the importance of each in different circumstances" (White 1950, 39). Anticipating Bardach, White argued for the prime necessity of identifying "generally valid rules" for large-scale action (p. 39).

The urge to set forth principles, though stifled temporarily, has regained popularity throughout the wider public management community, both in public administration (Bozeman and Straussman 1990; Rainey 1991; Denhardt 1993) and in public policy (Rumsfeld 1976; Chase and Reveal 1983; Lynn 1987a, 270–72; Behn 1988; Cohen 1988; Barzelay 1992, chaps. 7–8; Levin and Sanger 1994; Haass 1994). But White's advice, to push analysis further, has infrequently been heeded. As a result, there are relatively few rules or contingent conclusions (Rosenthal 1982; Hargrove and Glidewell 1990, chap. 3; Lynn 1990; Barzelay 1992, chap. 6) and relatively little interest in the debate. The public management community, it would seem, is laying foundations for practice deep in *unstable* principle.

---

9. Bendor and Hammond (1989), like Behn, draw an analogy between their methodological approach and learning chess. "Scholars trying to explain complex events are, like chess players, searching for solutions in very large problem spaces" (p. 49). Heuristic models assist scholars in discovering clues, and making rough guesses, about what part of the space to search first. Acquiring skill in chess, it would appear, is an inconveniently imprecise metaphor if Behn and Bendor and Hammond can draw contrary methodological advice from it.

The Analytical Manager

Here and now, or then and there? Experience and principles, or heuristics and rules? These are essentially empirical questions: which emphases turn out, on investigation, to be the more effective in improving practice? But they are seldom treated that way, perhaps because obtaining "hard" evidence on managerial effectiveness is so difficult.[10] The debate over how to create knowledge for practice has become essentially ideological. Proponents of different perspectives seldom engage each other around well-formed propositions, and they appeal to different audiences for approval. Advocates of more reductive approaches seek their support among practitioners. Advocates for more analytical approaches find comfort among academics.

There is, I believe, a reasonable basis for a choice of emphasis. The problem with reductionist views of public management is that they are palpably wrong in their premises and, for this reason, hardly a constructive guide to scholarship, teaching, and practice. A dispassionate study of cases, or the direct, open-minded observation of practice, will, I believe, reveal the extent to which public executives shape the institutional frameworks for policymaking and execution.

Virtually every significant issue on the agenda for political decision involves institutional/structural issues, and public executives participate in their deliberation and resolution. Virtually every significant executive assignment involves selecting the rules that govern the flow of information and ideas within and between agencies and that influence the content of both issue and decision agendas. Executives are the molders of contexts that will affect public policy in both the short and long runs. They inherit the structural legacies of predecessors, modify and redesign them, and leave legacies of their own to successors.

Scholars and teachers who assume away or neglect most of the

10. Exceptions are two empirical studies of the question, Do good managers grope along? One (Golden 1990) answers, "Yes, they do." The other (Straussman 1993) answers, "If they do, you don't know whether that's good or bad." It is questionable that this constitutes "depth."

vital institutional and intellectual content of public management are not only incorrect in their analysis of the nature of public management, they have walked into a trap of their own making. In ruling out or being dismissive of a role for instrumental or technical rationality as a dimension of effective practice, they have no where to go but toward the managerial Heart of Darkness in search of Kurtz, the legendary Public Manager cum Entrepreneur, Innovator, Risk Taker, Protector of the Constitution, and Civilizing Force, all courage and wisdom, possessing attributes that, alas, are virtually unteachable.

The trap can easily be avoided by taking a sufficiently broad perspective on public executive leadership. There is an insight from experience being missed, an idea infusing earlier classic works on executive leadership inspired by practice being forgotten.

In a remarkably prescient collection of essays (Gaus et al. 1936), Marshall Dimock sought to place administration in a broad context:

> Those of our permanent administrative officials *who have large responsibilities* should be competent to weigh social policies. They have to choose courses of conduct which will rebound to the public benefit.... [T]he field of public administration must emphasize the theory, the philosophy, the social problem of modern collective living instead of being content with the teaching of techniques of execution which appear to be ineffectual. (p. 129; italics added)

In *The Art of Judgment* (1983), Sir Geoffrey Vickers identifies skill as having five dimensions:

- Balancing, requiring a constant process of evaluating and appraisal, of risks, limitations, opportunities, and stakes.
- Integrating the incompatible, an "instrumental skill," says Vickers, and meaning "value creating" in contrast to "value claiming."
- Determining priorities—deciding what matters most in terms of consequences for the system—requiring both "a rare measure of mental discipline" and fine timing.
- Meeting immediate needs without sacrificing ideals or abandoning dreams.

- Formulating ideas ("the power to dream," in Vickers's words) with the potential to transform situations, to promote the spreading of ideas from their originators to others (pp. 111–12).

But "the most essential element," Vickers says, "is the skill to learn," to improve one's capacity for "not only instrumental judgment but also appreciative judgment, not only know-how but know what" (p. 112). This specific notion of learning echoes Andrew Abbott's (1988) concept of professionalism (to be discussed further in chapter 6) and can be expressed as follows: a executive who is professional in his or her approach has the ability to exercise mental discipline and the skill to learn, which can be said to mean the ability to apply a repertoire of abstractions to new situations and to redefine problems and tasks as justified by circumstances.

To illuminate further this notion of mental discipline and skill in the light of the needs of public management, it is instructive to review a largely forgotten appendix in Chester Barnard's *The Functions of the Executive* (1968). In an essay titled "The Mind in Everyday Affairs," Barnard, who is nothing if not experiential in his approach, argues for recognizing the importance of "non-logical processes" to success in management. It is these processes that give rise to timely reactions, intuitive insights, and, ultimately, good judgment. To "major executives," Barnard goes on, logical reasoning processes are necessary "but are disadvantageous if not in subordination to highly developed intuitional processes" (p. 320). It is well, then, to develop "the efficiency of the non-logical processes." How can this be done? Barnard's answer is "by conditioning the mind" through "stocking the mind properly" by study and by experience and, with the mind thus stocked, "in exercising the non-logical faculties" (p. 321).

The point is that study—stocking and conditioning the mind —is part of preparation for effective practice. Study refers to acquiring "facts, concepts, patterns" that the mind uses, largely intuitively, to formulate action. In this perspective, the issue is not whether to study conceptual frameworks as heuristics, but what heuristics to study and, in particular, what concepts will prepare the mind for its nonlogical, more intuitive work. In this vein, Bendor and Hammond (1989) note, in advocating the value of heuristic models, that "conceptual frameworks are not vacuous, i.e., they can significantly affect thinking without being either fully explicit or deductive." Training in heuristics, in other words, is the way to stock and condition the mind for its intuitive, creative work.

Philip Selznick's concept of institutional leadership embraces the notion of "the leader as educator" (1984, 157). The leader as educator, he argues, "requires an ability to interpret the role and character of the enterprise, to perceive and develop models for thought and behavior, and to find modes of communication that will inculcate general rather than merely partial perspectives." The goal of the leader is to achieve a state within the organization in which policy gains "spontaneous and reasoned support." Though he does not explicitly say so, the inescapable implication of Selznick's argument is that effective leadership is conceptual and thoughtful, involving rhetoric founded on reasoning.

It is true that the resolute advocate for "science" must concede the role of intuition not only in scientific work, as Gerald Holton (1988), among many others, has argued, in developing insights for action and for reflection in action. It is equally true that the resolute experientialist must likewise concede the role of study and the ability to conceptualize in order to penetrate surface impressions in heightening the value of experience. Failure to grasp the extent to which situations, actions, and events have a causal ordering, and that the public manager is a designer of order, is as primary an error as failure to grasp the extent to which luck and serendipity, accidents of timing, and the subtle feel for people and situations are similarly influential.

The fallacy underlying the concept of "reflective practitioner" and many of its derivatives popular in homiletic public management is that reason and intuition, calculation and creativity, problem solving and practice are somehow antithetical, as irreconcilable as Platonic and Aristotelian epistemologies. In contrast to the views of those such as Altshuler, Levin, and Nathan, the exercise of statecraft in performing the executive function in government is well served, even if not completely defined, by the development and use of critical analytical skills. Creating and applying an appropriate body of knowledge, it follows, is a necessary activity of university-based scholars and teachers in the field of public management.

5

KNOWLEDGE FOR
PRACTICE

We do not need proof or provable theses so much as we need questions and hypotheses which will stimulate insights among practitioners. The methodology of social science research can encourage
administrators to be more self-consciously analytical and reflective
about whatever art they believe they practice.

— Gordon R. Clapp

In managing the public's business, who *fails,* and why? A preoccupation with success, which has become de rigeur in public
management research, obscures a useful route to identifying
the essentials of thoughtful public management practice: analyzing
failure. Incompetent public managers are, after all, easier to identify
and, indeed, if public discontent is any indicator, far more numerous
than ones who succeed.

There are as many themes in the criticisms of public managers
as there are theories of success and failure. An ousted official described as "intense, unpredictable, and abrasive" may be succeeded
by one soon criticized as "aloof, distant, and indifferent to gritty details, more concerned with the public than with his subordinates,
demonstrating no dynamism, no zest, no verve, no panache." Criticized officials, it is often argued, "failed to provide a vision,"

"moved too slowly and cautiously," "failed to build a base of support," "alienated key supporters," "went by the rules instead of using common sense," and so on.

Such criticisms are persuasive: a politically astute, engaged, sensible visionary is surely to be preferred to any of the unfortunate incumbents depicted in the above slanders. One implication is that senior elected and appointed officials should make more carefully considered appointments to public executive posts than they do. It is puzzling why so many appointees, introduced to the public in a triumphant spirit, soon fail for reasons that a competent search ought to have foreseen.

Once on the job, what will even well-appointed officials be called on to think about and do? How will they handle the specific demands of their jobs? From this perspective, another theme, one more germane to the argument in this monograph, is heard in criticisms of public executives. One hears of officials who

- "Shoot from the hip" or decide on the basis of "gut reactions"
- Base their decisions on "which way the wind is blowing" or on the basis of simple expediency
- Take the advice of the last person who pleaded with them, are "over their heads," or are unable to "get on top of the problem"
- Get "bogged down in the details," cannot "find the handles" on an issue, or cannot make a decision or a tough call
- Are "lightweights" or fail to "do their homework"
- Compartmentalize their thinking, fail to see the relationships among seemingly disparate issues, or are inconsistent in explanation and action.

Officials who get tagged with these epithets are almost certain to be lacking in a basic skill: knowing how to exercise mental discipline on the job. Such officials are unable to ask good questions, to allocate their own or their staff's time efficiently in studying the issues, or to evaluate conflicting or poorly conceived evidence and arguments. They are unable to cope with substantive complexity or to penetrate the welter of details to identify essential issues. They do not grasp the ways in which apparently disparate issues are in fact interrelated.

As a result of low levels of intellectual skill, public executive performance may become disorganized or desultory or reactive. Public executives with inadequate mental preparation may be driven to seeking paths of least resistance through the daily morass of claims, irritants, and frustrations, to making snap judgments, deferring to someone else, procrastinating, or simply screwing up.

Competence in this sense means the ability to think systematically and clearly about complex or unfamiliar policy or organizational problems, then form an independent and competent view of the issues, alternatives, and likely consequences of different actions. The use of such ability occurs, moreover, in an unpredictable, distracting, and highly charged political environment. Competence means having confidence in one's ability to think and act sensibly in the face of uncertainty, incomplete information, multiple and competing objectives, value conflicts, and irresolvable disagreements over what should be done.

This characterization is, of course, an incomplete view of competence. As suggested earlier, executive shortcomings come in a great range of shades, as pale as simple inexperience, as dark as insufficiency of character. Moreover, the notion that "good managers can think straight and base action on thought" begs a basic question: how do we know that this is true? Evidence, as I have stressed all along, is lacking.

It is true, as James Q. Wilson has argued (see chapter 2), that executives must meet different mental and personal challenges depending on the type of agency they manage and the level of government at which they serve. Despite the lack of good evidence, it is hard to imagine that many jobs of consequence lack a substantive, analytical dimension, though the relative importance of this dimension will vary across situations.

The belief that, for public managers, "practice is analysis" is the premise for what follows for three reasons. Helping managers do well at thinking straight and acting in a thoughtful manner (1) is bound to produce better performance, all other things equal, in a way that having a more admirable character or more enlightened values will not; (2) is an appropriate goal for university-based education and training in a way that character and personality development are not; and (3) is essential to the creation of a viable concept of professionalism in public management in a way that a stress on personal beliefs and qualities is not.

Learning to Manage

When heading into the "learning to practice" thicket, it is important to recognize that the form that knowledge takes has significant implications for how difficult it is to learn and, presumably, who can be good at it.

Max Boisot (1986) has developed an analytic framework that is helpful in identifying learning issues. He begins with two assumptions: (1) "reality" is a social construction rather than an objective construct that is the same for all observers, and (2) organizations are systems of socially constructed and cognitively ordered meanings. For any individual in an organization, experience and action are based on a blend of tacit or uncodified knowledge and of structured or codified knowledge.

Both tacit and codified knowledge are regarded by actors within an organization as valid as they construct reality for themselves; they accept facts, suggestive interpretations, and intuitive feel as useful. Tacit knowledge, however, is perceived as inherently vague, ambiguous, and uncertain. As such, it is more difficult to communicate to others. Saying "trust me" is often used as a substitute for persuasion when acceptance of tacit knowledge is sought. Because of these properties of tacit knowledge, its acceptance depends on a sharing of expectations and values achieved through essentially social relationships that may take time to develop. Codified knowledge, in contrast, is more impersonal, associated less with proper socialization or experience than with skill in abstract thinking and linear reasoning. Saying "listen to me" may be effective with those who may resist proposals for lack of understanding.

An analysis of learning issues conceived in a similar spirit is that of Bolman and Deal (1991, 19).[1] They note that learning directed to recall or application is the easiest to accomplish. More difficult is learning that creates associations—analogies, metaphors—that will be recognized as valid in subsequent situations. The most difficult learning to master is the development of multiple *stencils* that frame and, when integrated artfully, give meaning to particular experience. The first type of learning may enable one to produce logical solutions to well-defined problems. When produced by the latter type of learning, a managerial act is a unique "work of art."

To summarize—and necessarily to oversimplify—the point, some types of knowledge are easier to come by, because they are more linear and impersonal, than others. Considerations of deference and trust do not intrude. We may call such knowledge "scientific" or "technocratic." Uncodified, undiffused knowledge (e.g., the tacit, intuitive knowledge of a wise and experienced manager who communicates primarily in face-to-face forums and by the example of behavior) is difficult to master in any conventional sense because considerations other than the literal and the logical are involved. We may call such difficult-to-acquire mastery "artistic."

For codified, technocratic knowledge, the university course, the supervised workshop, and the problem set or other formal assignment, all emphasizing individual goal achievement, may be the most efficient approaches to learning. For tacit, artistic knowledge, mentorship, apprenticeship, and internship tending toward socialization —and perhaps prolonged on-the-job experience—are likely to be the most efficient ways to promote learning. Where both types of knowledge, or their subtle integration, are required for success, vicarious experience in simulated work situations featuring both social and intellectual demands—for example, case discussions requiring the application of a mix of analytic frameworks—may be the appropriate approach to learning.

Administrative Art and Social Science

How can scholars and teachers in the field of public management

1. Bolman and Deal acknowledge the ideas of Broudy (1981).

contribute to managerial competence founded on exercising mental discipline "on line"? What are the tools and materials—the heuristics—of the manager as analytical craft worker? How does one learn to mix the technocratic and the artistic in ways that lead to effective management?

Thus conceived, a public manager's basic tool kit will necessarily contain a variety of models and conceptual frameworks together with rules for their application; intellectual constructs that, when used as lenses through which to interpret messy facts, reveal fundamental issues that must be resolved; and stylized facts, counterfactuals, and other intellectual instruments that expose fallacious reasoning and uncover pitfalls blocking task completion or outcome achievement. The manager becomes a trained investigator, able to examine competing claims, to interrogate experts, and to resolve uncertainty in a reasoning way.

Several veins of inquiry originating within the social science community seem to have considerable promise as sources of explanatory heuristics bearing on the motivations, strategies and choices of public managers. A number originate in the use of rational choice theories to model economic, political, and social behavior. Sociologists are responsible for two others: the so-called new institutionalism and network theory and its applications. Psychology provides theories of decision making, bounded rationality, and the social psychology of organizational behavior. The following sketches are intended to be illustrative, not definitive: a place to begin, not to end up.

Gamesmanship

An important problem in public management is choosing strategies in the light of the choices that participants in a multiactor world might make. The metaphorical use of "game" and "gamesmanship" has long been popular among students of political life. More formally, the prisoners' dilemma has been widely used to demonstrate that rational actors can produce socially nonoptimal outcomes.[2]

2. Russell Hardin (1982) has demonstrated that Olson's (1971) collective action problem is an *n*-person prisoners' dilemma.

Noncooperative game theory in general provides a conceptual apparatus for understanding social outcomes that are jointly determined by participants whose own strategic choices are based on a structure of payoffs that is conditional on the choices of other participants.

An understanding of strategies and payoffs would be valuable in appraising the prospects for cooperation in particular cases. An important strand of research has revealed that the prospect of repeated interactions ("the shadow of the future") tends to induce cooperation even in noncooperative games. Gary Miller has observed that the Folk Theorem (according to which there are multiple equilibria in repeated games) "forces an awareness of the multiple possibilities of political life, and requires attention to a set of social phenomena that allow political actors to coordinate on one of the many equilibrium possibilities available" (1990, 61).

More recently, attention has been directed at games with communication and at the possibilities for "coordinated strategies" even in a single play of a prisoners' dilemma. A related idea is that of "nested games," in which the outcomes of particular games are influenced, via coordinated strategies or interdependent payoffs, with the outcomes of adjacent games.

Game theory, therefore, is a potentially useful source of explanatory heuristics for the managerial problem of making strategic choices (1) when a manager is simultaneously accountable to several actors, or operating in multiactor fields; or (2) when a manager is seeking results through hierarchies involving separate but interdependent interactions (e.g., between division and the field, the field and the direct service worker, the direct service worker and the client); or (3) when a manager is engaged in a series of repeated interactions or must predict the behavior of other actors who are so engaged (Lynn 1993).

Agency and Performance

Securing reliable task performance from agents is another common problem in public management. Specifically, the problems arise from two possibilities: (1) hidden action, the inability of a principal to observe the extent to which an agent's actions are diligent in compliance with the principal's expectations; and (2) hidden information, an agent possessing information not possessed by the principal and the opportunity to use it in a manner inconsistent with the principal's expectations (Arrow 1985). The problems arise when an agent's preferences or incentives are such that reliable performance cannot be assumed by the principal.

Principal-agent theory has given rise to an extensive formal analytics of performance contracting. Extensions of the basic model have been made to include, for example, problems associated with multiple principals, multiple agents, multiple tasks, and monitoring and enforcement problems. Nevertheless, attempts to use the theory to explain real-world behavior have led Arrow (1985) to observe that its explanatory power is relatively weak. "[The] cost of communication, variety and vagueness of monitoring, and [existence of] socially mediated rewards" are beyond usual boundaries of economic analysis. Bendor (1990) adds another caveat: the assumption, necessary to principal-agent theory, that a principal can precommit to an incentive scheme may be an inappropriate assumption concerning political commitment to policies (p. 391).

Arrow concludes, however, that "it may ultimately be one of the greatest accomplishments of the principal-agent literature to provide some structure for the much-sought goal of integrating these [non-economic] elements with the impressive structure of economic analysis" (1985, 50). Arrow's remark suggests that if the theory is weak as a tool of empirical social science, it may nonetheless be powerful as a source of explanatory heuristics that integrate numerous factors of interest in a conceptually organized way.

Several contributions suggest the insights that are possible when the problem is the common one of "incentive incompatibility" between principals and agents.[3] Holmstrom and Milgrom (1991), for example, have reached the important result that, when agents have tasks with many dimensions of varying complexity, paying a fixed salary regardless of measured performance can be superior to performance contracts, which, because they are incomplete with respect

3. In addition to sources cited in the text, see Dunleavy (1985, 1991).

to all relevant aspects of the job, unduly distort agency incentives. In a related vein, Hammond and Miller (1985) conclude that when

> the capabilities of the workers must be measured[, they have] an incentive to manipulate the measurements.... The behavior encouraged by formal incentive systems ("Cooperate for the good of the organization") may also run counter to that encouraged by promotion systems ("Distinguish yourself from your colleagues"). (p. 35)

This reasoning would suggest caution when advising managers to establish measurable goals and performance contracts.

Patrick Dunleavy has produced insights of a similar nature by identifying collective action problems that exist within bureaucracies and that influence the behavior of the organization. He argues that "utility-maximizing bureaucrats are empirically more likely to be orientated towards the intrinsic character of their work tasks" to pursue what he calls "bureau-shaping strategies" than to strategies that benefit the bureau as a whole (Dunleavy 1985, 300). He goes on to argue that

> in contrast to conventional public administration with its stress on describing actors' behavior in terms of the motivations and intentions of biographically realistic individuals, economic models offer a partial account of how actors operate as bearers-of-roles-in-organizations.... [A] public choice model can be read as an analysis of the situational logic facing any instrumental actor in a given role, with no necessary connection to the voluntaristic and dispositional style of explanation used by [other writers]. (p. 327)

The use of such conceptual frameworks to study the incentive effects of goals is surely a better basis for advising practitioners than ideologically justified advocacy of performance measurement as an unexceptionable principle.

Institutional Design
How can public managers contribute to the creation of institutional arrangements that serve the aims of public policy? How should they seek to shape their mandates? Based in large part on transaction-

cost economics (transaction costs are the costs of measuring and enforcing agreements), analysts of institutions are attempting to show how institutional arrangements arise to create order and reduce uncertainty in economic and political exchange (North 1991, 97). "A transaction cost theory of politics is built on the assumptions of costly information, of subjective models on the part of the actors to explain their environment, and of imperfect enforcement of agreements. Choices employing such models result in high political transaction costs that make political markets very imperfect" (North 1990, 355). Institutions establish transaction costs at a moment of time and determine the evolution of political and economic change.

Using a transaction cost framework, Heckathorn and Maser (1990) address the question, "If the government is in some measure autonomous, ... how does it come to be involved in some coercive activities and not others?" They "view government activities, including statutes and the organizations that administer them, as long-term contracts that people negotiate to economize on the costs of decision making" (p. 1103). The form of the contract depends on the problem giving rise to these costs. If the problem is lack of coordination, the contract will call for planning and information-dissemination services. If the problem is conflict, the contract will call for bargaining and resource-allocation services. If the problem is defection or a failure of collective action, the contract will call for regulatory and enforcement services. Thus the missions and forms of institutions, and, presumably, the nature of managerial roles, are influenced by the character of underlying breakdown of private attempts to cooperate.

An ingenious contribution by William Ouchi (1980) begins with the observation that "transactions costs arise principally when it is difficult to determine the value of the goods or service." Three distinct institutional forms address this problem: markets, bureaucracies, and clans. Markets work when all necessary information is conveyed in prices and a norm of reciprocity (value given for value received) prevails. When contracts cannot cover all contingencies or uncertainties, bureaucracies arise to permit the substitution of employment relations (an incomplete contract) for spot or contingent-claims contracts. A norm of authority is added to the norm of reciprocity, and necessary information is conveyed in rules. But "when tasks become highly unique, completely integrated, or ambiguous for other reasons, then even bureaucratic mechanisms fail (Ouchi 1980, 134–35). A clan mechanism may solve the control problem if a system of shared values and beliefs, conveyed through traditions, rituals, and symbols, can be established.

> Bureaucratic organizations exist because, under certain specifiable conditions, they are the most efficient means for an equitable mediation of transactions between parties.... [M]arket and clan organizations exist because each of them, under certain conditions, offers the lowest transactions cost. (p. 140)

Wilkins and Ouchi (1983) argue that managing organizational cultures is equivalent to creating clanlike mechanisms for organizational control:

> If the transaction cost perspective is usefully accurate, clan forms of control will be less efficient than competing bureaucratic or market forms in governing transactions where the level of complexity or uncertainty is relatively low or moderate. The clan may require the development and maintenance of too much social agreement to be efficient under less ambiguous transactional conditions. On the other hand, the clan will be more efficient, as we have shown, under conditions of ambiguity, complexity, and interdependence of transactions. (p. 477)

Susan Rose-Ackerman (1986b), in contrast, says that while her own bias "is to control bureaucratic conduct through arm's length incentive payments that do not interfere directly with the details of individual behavior," it is also true that "considerable risks attend a system based entirely on trust and professionalism" (p. 150). She concludes that "the creative development of performance-based incentive systems should be a high priority for bureaucratic reform" but that "a workable scheme of economic incentives depends on the measurability of output, on who can observe this output, and on the risk aversion of officials."[4]

4. This proposition rests heavily on a number of simplifying assumptions. See Rose-Ackerman (1986b, 150, 133 n. 3).

Ostrom, Schroeder, and Wynne (1993) have shown how an institutional analysis based on transaction costs can illuminate the consequences of alternative ways of creating rural infrastructure. (See also Ostrom [1986].) Is it appropriate, in the light of such analyses, for public executives to propose (as the Clinton administration did in the case of community development banking) replicating a particular structural model judged to have been successful in one location in numerous other locations? Scholars of institutions are able to show how different types of rules shape outcomes: who participates, toward what ends, and without what likely consequences.

The nonprofit organization, that is, one formed with a charitable purpose and subject to a nondistribution constraint (perhaps thought of as a kind of clan), is an economic response to "contract failure," a situation in which the transaction costs of ensuring that charitable goals are in fact carried out are so high that markets do not form (Hansmann 1986). The nonprofit organization inspires trust in donors by promising that any temporary excess of revenues over costs will be redirected toward the mission of the organization, rather than dispersed as dividends or bonuses.

Thus institutional forms are not arbitrary or exogenous. They are endogenous to the process of political choice. Public managers can be conceived as participating purposefully in this choice process. They can be educated to understand the issues and alternatives and their implications for how they should manage.

In an organization producing goods or services, technologies are used to transform inputs into outputs. The transformation process requires structures to organize and assign work and responsibility: these structures define the organization's technical core. The nature of these structures depends in part on the nature of the outputs. Are they manufactured goods, individualized services, or collective goods? Are they standardized, customized, or one of a kind?

In the case of manufactured goods, technologies are likely to be "hard," and technological change will lead to structural change. In the case of services, technologies are likely to be "soft"—embedded in the organization's structures—and the causal arrow may be reversed: structural change is required for technological change.

Organizations tend to defend their technical core (or primary work system) against exogenous change. In the case of soft technologies, where efficiency gains are hard to demonstrate, bringing about structural change in an organization may be particularly difficult.

Social Preferences and Accountability

To whom, or to what principals, are managerial agents accountable? How much autonomy do they possess? It is conventional wisdom that (1) managers, especially senior executives, are accountable to multiple interests; and (2) there is a measure of autonomy or discretion in virtually every position. Analytically, the problems of discretion and accountability are addressed from several perspectives.

Based on the logic of collective action, for example, Mancur Olson (1971) conceived the role of the political entrepreneur, often an executive, who, for various reasons, seeks to elicit or sustain effort in behalf of the production and continuing provision of collective goods (pp. 174–78). This theory accords a rather powerful position to public executives. Against the view that rational individuals reveal their preferences through the prices they are willing to pay in markets or through their votes, the logic of collective action suggests that, in a large number of important cases, potential beneficiaries of governmental action may have no incentive to reveal their preferences at all unless specifically induced to do so by an entrepreneur. As architects of such inducements, public executives are significant actors in arranging collective outcomes, a role that decisively sets them apart from their private-sector counterparts, whose role is to identify and respond to (or create) market demand (Lynn 1992, 5).

Public choice economics provides a different perspective on executive roles and discretion. Members of an enacting coalition face an agency problem: securing compliance from bureaucratic agencies with the intentions of the members. Mathew McCubbins, Roger Noll, and Barry Weingast (1987, 1989) are concerned with what they call "bureaucratic drift" and with how enacting coalitions can design administrative arrangements and engage in monitoring to forestall it. (They support their arguments, incidentally, with extensive and detailed case material.) Horn and Shepsle (1989) identify McCubbins, Noll, and Weingast's most important contribution as follows:

> The authors point out not only that the policy implemented by bu-
> reaucratic agents can differ from that enacted by the coalition (bu-
> reaucratic drift), but also that conflicts-of-interest among the mem-
> bers of this coalition may prevent them from effectively employing
> standard ex post corrective devices—budgetary sanctions, hearings,
> and so on—to reinstate the enacted policy. . . . [Unfortunately], nei-
> ther the specificity of the enabling legislation, denial of agent flexi-
> bility, nor participation by interested parties is necessarily optimal
> or self-fulfilling; therefore, they do not ensure agent compliance. (p.
> 502)

Indeed, bureaucratic agents can exploit this multiple principals problem to their advantage.

Public choice frameworks, especially when they incorporate
principal-agent theory, can prove highly suggestive of the kinds of
dynamics that affect the ongoing shaping and execution of legislative
mandates and that shape executive roles. It should be clear that accountability is, at best, a complex concept, highly dependent on political context and irreducibly discretionary.

Policy Politics

Legislators create imperfect or incomplete mandates. Thus bureaucratic agencies have substantial discretion to "complete" the process
of making policy (Brodkin 1986, 1987–88, 1990). While an agency's
employees may recognize and attempt to carry out a democratically
sanctioned program, they may also pursue particular "bureaucratic"
interests, although they may disguise this "undemocratic" activity as
the legitimate exercise of expertise or neutral competence. In fact,
agency employees, especially at lower levels, are in a strong position
to pursue their own interests because of the nature of bureaucratic
structures; information asymmetries and collective action problems
inside an agency mean that control by legislators and top-level executives is necessarily imperfect and costly to improve (Mechanic
1962).

The questions facing public management analysts are, When is
the autonomy of lower level personnel a problem? When is it a solution? How can "accountability problems" be overcome (1) by legis-

lative bodies, (2) political executives, and (3) middle-level managers? Gruber (1987) suggests several approaches: participation, client or customer relations, defining the public's interest, formal accountability, and self-control. Solutions are likely to depend on the particulars of a given context.

Leadership

What is the essential nature of political leadership? In a masterful monograph, Gary Miller (1990) demonstrates the general impossibility of constructing a correct set of incentives for shaping agent behavior. "Hierarchies can go part of the way toward correctly aligning individual and group incentives. But ... no budget-balancing incentive system in a hierarchy can perfectly align individual and group incentives." He concludes, therefore, that

> managers who can induce norms of cooperation and trust among employees can realize more of the gains from team production than can managers who rely on formal incentive systems only.... [Chester] Barnard's description of the executive's responsibility to elicit an expectation of mutual sacrifice and provide an example of morality sounds very much a formula for successful play of repeated prisoners' dilemma games. It is also a description of the kind of active political leadership that transcends the limits of mechanical management. (p. 214)

Formal modelers have produced other impossibility theorems, or proofs that such intuitively desirable criteria as decentralization, flexibility, and consistent orderings of choices are internally inconsistent (Bendor 1991, 399–403). Integrating such results with the Folk Theorem reinforces the notion that even in a world of rational actors, leaders' strategies may be decisive in directing commitments away from impossible goals, establishing realistic premises or organizational designs, and formulating missions that reconcile competing ideals.

The New Institutionalism

Sociologists have long held as a matter of principle that individual behavior cannot be viewed solely or even primarily as a matter of calculation in the light of a reduced set of factors. "Social" constructs such as roles, rules, norms, and expectations constrain individual choice (Powell and DiMaggio 1991). As Jane Fountain (1994) puts it, "the new institutionalism in political science and sociology represents the individual as a boundedly rational, culturally based 'practical' actor who has economic as well as noneconomic goals and whose actions are embedded in both social structures and ongoing social relationships" (p. 271).

Institutions can be conceptualized as regimes of rules that subsume "the beliefs, paradigms, codes, cultures, and knowledge that support roles and routines" (March and Olsen 1989, 22). Individual choice in an institutional setting, then, is a matter of matching the interpretation of the situation with appropriate norms or rules governing situations interpreted as such. Choice, then, is a matter both of cognition (and perhaps of calculation) and of obligation, duty, or collegiality.

Other institutional theories attend to the relationships between organizations and their environments and, in particular, to an organization's sources of legitimacy and external support. Maintenance of these relationships is apt to become codified in the form of rituals, myths, and ceremonies that may well have become dissociated from their original, perhaps highly rational, justifications. On the one hand, institutions so legitimized may prove to be highly resistant to change. On the other hand, institutions may come under pressure to adapt to changing, perhaps ephemeral expectations concerning appropriate missions, practices, and structures. For example, popular beliefs that "good" organizations (e.g., successful corporations) are following the latest management doctrines may translate into pressures on dissimilar organizations to embrace such doctrines, with the organizations thus becoming more isomorphic but without a contextually justified rationale.

Economic and technical considerations (e.g., transaction costs) determine the "original" form of organizations. But organizational forms may persist over time even when they are no longer "economical," especially when there is little or no competition. They are sustained by traditionalizing forces, such as the vesting of interests and the crystallization of ideologies. Organizations come to represent "property rights," that is, the rights of employees and stakeholders to participate in decisions and resource allocations.

According to Stinchcombe (1986), proposals to restructure organizations can be ranked in difficulty from "elementary administrative organizations" (which are rarely altogether free from tensions) to difficult reorganizations of property rights. The greater the difficulty of the change, (1) the more it must be legitimated by external forces; (2) the more concentration of power at the center, enthusiasm, and extraordinary leadership are necessary to bring it about; and (3) the more costly it will be.

For organizations (such as schools), or complex systems of organizations (such as school systems), in which (1) participants (teachers, principals, administrators, parents, community residents) have different, often conflicting, goals (goal incongruence), and (2) performance evaluation (determining whether the organization is efficient and effective) is inherently difficult (performance ambiguity), an organization's survival is best ensured by adopting formal structures and practices conforming to societal expectations as to how such organizations should look and function.

In such organizations, formal structures and rules are not solutions to coordination and control problems, nor do they reflect the rationalizing of exchange relationships with the environment. Instead, one observes loose coupling among the organization's subunits and reliance on a logic of confidence, good faith, and best effort as a substitute for reliance on formal systems of coordination and accountability. These formal systems serve a different purpose: reassuring interested constituencies that all is well, often by imitating the structures and practices of other organizations widely regarded as effective (isomorphism with environmental institutions).

Thus, in this view, organizations such as schools and school systems become institutionalized social structures and effectiveness is a socially constructed phenomenon with the purpose of maintaining societal support and ensuring survival.

Networks
Network analysis emphasizes relationships among actors, administrative units, or organizations, with the importance of individuals as

persons in their own right seen largely as epiphenomenal. Network theorists maintain that "what is really interesting and important about social structures and their embedded processes is not the presumed independent behavior of individuals, but instead the ways in which those individuals are influenced and constrained by their social relations to act in certain ways" (Schumm 1990). Network concepts are used to characterize structures of relationships, including the nature and extent of communication and influence. The properties of networks are used to account for their aggregate behavior and influence.

Network theory is a potentially valuable complement to both rational and normative theories of intra- and interorganizational relationships. In particular, network models facilitate analysis of how informal communications amend and rearrange formal hierarchical and peer relationships and reallocate resources (Knoke 1990). For example, actors are likely to depend on network forms of resource allocation under conditions of ambiguity and uncertainty that defeat rational means of control and communication (Powell 1990). Once a stable network structure is achieved, it "becomes a fact of organizational life" (Knoke 1990, 109).

Network concepts have significant implications for the management of change, for the creation of coalitions, for negotiation and the resolution of conflict, for evaluation and the monitoring of organizational and interorganizational activity, and for understanding the sources of organizational power and the significance of influence processes. Thus network theory is a source of valuable heuristics for understanding some of public management's most generic tasks.

The Cognitive/Emotional Actor[5]

Individuals differ widely in how they process information. They differ in the types and complexity of the structures they use to order and simplify reality and in the ways by which they create, modify, or validate those structures (i.e., learn).

Whatever their learning styles, individuals in decision-making and choice situations will be seeking to fulfill certain cognitive and

5. This section incorporates material from Lynn (1980, 12–14).

emotional needs. They typically strive for certainty, stability, simplicity, and consistency in their interpretations of reality and their beliefs about the world. They will employ a variety of psychological and other means to protect themselves from threats to these highly valued states of mind.

Confronted with complexity, conflict, and uncertainty, a decision maker may experience genuine stress, frustration, anxiety, and self-doubt. These emotional responses to the situation may not be evident to staff or colleagues, but their underlying presence may explain much of the decision-maker's observed behavior. In the face of uncertainty, and the realization that calculated risks must be taken, a decision maker may procrastinate, hoping that something better will turn up. Alternatively, the decision maker may make a decision prematurely, hoping to eliminate the stressful situation, or decide in effect to see only the advantages of one particular course of action and only the disadvantages of others, thus minimizing the painfulness of the choice and the perceived magnitude of the risks. Individuals may adopt a wide variety of rationalizations that distort or bias the assessment of available information, all toward the end of increasing confidence that the chosen course of action is clearly the right one.

The successive application of four distinctive "theories" of organizations—structural, human resource, political, and symbolic—will enable managers (and management analysts) to formulate better management analyses and strategies than if only one or two frames are used. The appropriate mix of frames will vary from situation to situation, however.

Reasoning for Management

Suppose a manager's mind is, as Chester Barnard advises, stocked with applicable heuristics. What is heuristically conditioned managerial reasoning like? This style of reasoning can be illustrated by comparing the advice emanating from a reliance on tacit, experiential learning with advice that has a more analytic foundation. Following is a set of circumscribed, partial arguments chosen to illustrate the value of the notion that good managers can think straight.

Working the Seams

In his excellent paper "Graduate Education in Public Management: Working the Seams of Government," Richard Elmore (1986) argues that public managers are *agents* of constitutional officials who know how to work the *seams* of government: the boundaries between administrative agencies and legislative bodies, between levels of government, between administrative agencies and interest groups, the media, and the like. Skill in working these seams, he argues, requires, among other things, mastery of a *technical core* of analytic and managerial skills.

The notion of a seam is a useful metaphor. It will give students in graduate programs a way of intuitively understanding the sources of the problems that preoccupy public managers. One might well leave it at that: think "seams." Elmore's metaphor raises deeper questions, however. What kinds of issues arise at the seams of government, and how do such issues manifest themselves as demands on a public manager's time and talents? Is this metaphor more useful, or more descriptively accurate, or more intellectually suggestive, than other ways of characterizing the problem of public management?

Scholars and teachers have produced numerous metaphors designed to identify generic problems of public management. I argue, for example (Lynn 1982), that public managers can be seen viewed participants in multiple, continuing *games* occurring at different levels of government. Vickers (1983) postulates that the executive function "consists partly in maintaining the actual course of affairs in line with ... governing relations as they happen to be at the time and partly in modifying ... governing relations so as to 'maximize the values' ... which can be realized through the pursuit of these relationships, whilst keeping the aggregate of activities within the bounds of possibility" (p. 27). In other words, public managers maintain and modify *governing relations* in order to maximize value. Lindblom views public executives as participants in a process of *partisan mutual adjustment*. Heclo (1977, 1979) views them as *strangers* who participate in *issue networks*. Edelman (1964, 1988) views them as actors in *public dramas* in which words and actions have symbolic value. Cohen, March, and Olsen (1972) see them as actors in *organized anarchies* whose decision making takes place in *garbage cans.* Kaufman (1981) sees them as elements of a *system of organic interdependence tending toward stasis* (in contrast to a system shaped by centrifugal forces.)

Each metaphor is likely to yield different insights concerning management in particular cases. Kaufman points out, for example, that the metaphor of stasis logically leads to decentralization, whereas the metaphor of centrifugal forces leads to centralization of authority. Partisan mutual adjustment suggests a negotiation logic whose goal is incremental change. Organized anarchies suggest a logic of opportunism and flexibility. If they are to serve a useful educational purpose, metaphors used as heuristics require that their claims to usefulness be justified empirically in important classes of cases.

Elmore's metaphors—agents, seams, technical core—suggests, moreover, points of contact with a number of more formal intellectual approaches or traditions of inquiry. In viewing the public manager as either an agent for constitutional authority or as principal for employees, for example, the problem of public management becomes one of securing reliable behavior from subordinates-as-agents through specifying appropriate behavior, creating incentives (and disincentives) to induce appropriate behavior, and the monitoring and policing of the resulting behavior. Seams suggests public managers working at the boundaries between organizations viewed as open systems and their environments, thus invoking the intellectual structures and research findings of open systems, contingency, and resource dependence theories (Scott 1992).[6] Finally, the concept of core activity implies that every organization has a primary task, or a primary work system, which is the raison d'etre for the organization and which is the source of legitimacy or meaning for the organization's employees (Scott 1992). As I have shown elsewhere (Lynn 1985, 1987a), the concept of core activity can be used to evaluate systematically the performances of public managers against a criterion other than their self-reported goals and achievements.

6. A study in this tradition concluded, for example, that mayors account for less than 10 percent of the variation in most city budget expenditures, a finding with interesting implications (Salancik and Pfeffer 1977).

To say "work the seams" may or may not have heuristic value. Why not offer the actual or would-be practitioner a repertoire of heuristics for ordering messy reality and suggest rules for their applicability?

Achieving the Goal

In a well-crafted teaching case, "Homestead Air Force Base," Behn (1991) describes how Colonel William Gorton increased the productivity of his U.S. Air Force tactical fighter wing by establishing a clear, measurable goal and managing so as to achieve it. Based on the data in this case, Behn has distilled "Some Principles of Public Management," which he provides as a handout to participants at the conclusion of case discussion.[7] These principles are reproduced in table 5.1.

TABLE 5.1

HOMESTEAD AIR FORCE BASE: SOME PRINCIPLES
OF PUBLIC MANAGEMENT

I. Managing for performance
  1. Establish an overall mission for the organization.
  2. Create specific goals to measure the achievement of the mission.
  3. Monitor progress personally and frequently.
  4. Reward success publicly.
  5. Be vigilant for distortions.
  6. Modify mission, goals, monitoring, or rewards to correct defects in organizational behavior.

Continued . . .

7. Behn's own account of how he approaches the analysis of cases is in Behn (1993). There he says, "The practitioners of case-analysis research will never be able to prove that they are right. They will not even be able to prove that their work is helpful, for even the testimony of managers who find the insights of case analyses useful does not constitute proof. But at least those engaged in case-analysis research will know that they are asking important questions" (p. 53).

II. Gorton and Creech on management
   1. Appearance is critical.
   2. Pay attention to details.
   3. Create friendly, productive, controlled competition—competition against a goal so that every unit can win, not competition against other units that produces only one winner.
   4. The program has to be visible. You don't get credit for an accomplishment unless you make a prior commitment to doing it.
   5. Create ownership: nobody ever washed a rental car.
   6. The staff should serve the line. But how can you get the staff to focus on the job of serving the line and thus serving the agency's mission?

III. Analyzing management strategies
   1. A general management strategy can apply in a wide variety of specific—and seemingly very different—management situations.
   2. Be careful about employing any particular application of a general management strategy to a new situation. Rather, adapt it to the specific circumstances of the situation.

IV. Total Quality Management
   1. To improve performance, a manager must engage everyone in the organization in the task of improving the organization's product.
   2. To become an excellent organization requires continuous improvement.
   3. It is most efficient to do it right the first time rather than check up later.
   4. Managers need to get the people within the organization—particularly those who work in support positions—to understand who their customers are.
   5. Quality must have explicit measures of success.
   6. Total Quality Management is designed to improve results.

———————

In contrast to this by-now familiar (and virtually unexceptionable) "list of principles," what follows is a distillation of insights produced by graduate students based on having applied a variety of conceptual heuristics to the data in the case.

- Colonel Gorton had to plan far enough in advance to ensure that the goals he set—a specific number of sorties (training flights) each month—were achievable and would not be thrown off by events beyond his control. An unforseen event could destroy the viability of the goals system in the eyes of Gorton's people and thereby undermine the engine of productivity he was trying to build. The credibility of his goals was enhanced by his having involved base personnel who would be affected by them and who would advise him on their practicality in the analysis leading to goal selection.

- Since each aircraft maintenance unit was attached to a squadron, each crew was attached to an airplane, and everyone was connected to the possibility of earning a day off if a certain number of sorties was reached, an engine of incentive and accountability was created. Thus individual pride, responsibility, and self-interest were tied to the goals of the organization: a powerful solution to the principal-agent problem.

- Unless closely monitored, subordinates may respond to performance incentives by emphasizing the quantity of output rather than the more complex purpose of the activity. Thus Colonel Gorton had to watch his teams, as he put it, "like a hawk" to ensure that nobody was "fudging out there."

- Colonel Gorton used symbols and the force of his presence to reinforce his intentions and lessen uncertainty and misunderstanding concerning his mission and goals. His public, enthusiastic commitment to the new incentive system and the constant reminder of the symbols gave it credibility.

- In being willing to risk his own relationship with his superiors in the name of quality and safety by temporarily stopping all flights at the base until safety issues were addressed, Gorton sent a strong signal to his people that the numbers were a measure of performance but not the essence of what was to be accomplished.

- Analysis might have been, but was not, employed to determine if the real goal of the base—training pilots—could be achieved more effectively by means other than increasing the number of sorties. What are the factors that determine the learning of pilots? What is the most efficient way to deliver the needed training? Failure to address such questions reveals the downside of a strong organizational culture such as an air force tactical fighter wing: some valid questions do not get asked.

- Gorton implicitly took advantage of the military command traditions that affected all personnel at the base. His particular approach might not work, or work in the same way, in other contexts, where the legitimacy of hierarchy and command cannot be taken for granted.

The virtue of such insights is that they expose the kind of thinking on which effective action is grounded and the extent to which such thinking is explicitly contextual. A teacher might well leave it at that. If the format of "principles" is thought to be an effective pedagogical device, an analytically grounded approach to addressing this management case might lead to a list of principles different from Behn's:

- Choose goals that careful analysis reveals are clearly related to, and achievable through, enhanced employee effort; do not expose employees to risks of failure over which they have no control.

- Recognize that goal-oriented incentive systems are not self-enforcing; managers must reinforce their intent and meaning through reiteration and symbolic reinforcement, exemplary acts and behaviors. Otherwise, goal distortion is likely.

- Do not allow narrowly drawn goals to distract attention from more fundamental purposes. Performance data will not tell the entire story. Effort is needed to get behind them. Performance indicators are just that—indicators—and not performance itself.

- Structural change, motivational measures, careful analysis, and flexible and inspirational leadership are mutually reinforcing; no one of them alone will suffice.
- Thus, good management means
    a. minimizing uncertainty concerning the organization's objectives and appropriate ways to achieve them;
    b. providing a certain prospect of rewards tied to repeated, observable achievements;
    c. establishing strong norms of cooperation, reinforced by effective monitoring, to motivate lower-level personnel;
    d. tying the manager's own reputation to how well the organization performs.

Choosing principles is a matter of taste, but I believe the second list, derived from the application of conceptual frameworks to the data in the case, is more likely than the first list to prepare practitioners for exercising mental discipline.

Welfare to Work

Perhaps no field of public management is more in need of insightful knowledge than that concerned with assisting the poor to become self-sufficient through work. In a book based on a survey of experience with implementing the Family Support Act's JOBS program, Nathan (1993) argues that public officials must give more attention to management if they are to meet the legitimate expectations of citizens. From experience in implementing domestic policies, he derives ten lessons (133–36) for managing welfare-to-work programs:

- Implementation should get more attention.
- Strike while the iron is hot.
- Institutions matter.
- People matter, too.
- Stick around.
- Set goals that can be used as the basis for rewards and punishments.
- Avoid being mired in details.
- Respect careerists but watch them.

- Be shrewd about relations with the legislature.
- Do what has to be done.

In Bardach's *Improving the Productivity of JOBS Programs* (1993), effective management of the same kinds of programs boils down to "goal-setting and outcome measurement" (p. 58). His advice as to how a manager should behave—conveyed in a suggested speech for delivery by a newly appointed public manager to the inner circle of subordinate managers—reflects, he says, "conventional academic wisdom about organizational change." A key paragraph is the following:

> We should continue to focus on the employment goal, but we should be stretching ourselves to achieve more—without distorting our purpose by working only with the most employable clients. If we expect more of ourselves, chances are better that we'll achieve more. (p. 58)

Bardach's is an upbeat, primarily normative stance, reflecting a tacit sense of "wisdom" and "values." His intellectual resources prominently include Behn's *Leadership Counts* (1991). He also comes close to endorsing a "business has the answers" view by favorably citing Osborne and Gaebler (1992) and Barzelay (1992), where emulation of successful corporate reinvention is a leitmotif. In general, the research literature he cites seems to fall within what Bolman and Deal (1991) would call the "human resources frame"; he appears in his concluding message to make little use of their political, structural, or symbolic frames.

How useful are Nathan's principles or Bardach's narrative "conclusion" to managing programs? I doubt that practicing managers will find more than superficial inspiration when confronting specific management problems. Bardach might have been far more useful had he concluded by applying his own, much more textured and contingent thinking on management. Earlier in his monograph, he draws on his own (with Kagan) *Regulatory Unreasonableness* (1982). Noting that JOBS incorporates contradictory features—being nice and being tough—he says that "because the threat of sanctions (that is, grant reduction) can provoke resistance, it should be used economically" and "'manditoriness' is a medium for communicating norms of responsibility as well as threatening sanctions." He also notes the fundamental importance of how rewards are designed and administered. If not done well, he says, "all the problems associated with goal-setting and performance measurements will also be magnified" (p. 46). Donahue (1989), Lax and Sebenius (1986), and Kelman (1990) are cited as intellectual supports, though for specific confirming commentary rather than for the logic of their analytic frameworks.

Bardach might have concluded with the following advice to managers:

- Administering a JOBS program requires you to manage a fundamental tension: between being nice and being tough. Encouraging explicit self-consciousness of this tension among your people will make it more likely that you can manage it. When confronting perplexing client behavior, ask, "Why is this person acting this way?" before reaching a judgment.
- One way to establish the appropriate orientation of service workers (or contractors) toward clients is to set performance goals and monitor them. "Nice" or "tough" can then be discussed in relation to a valid purpose, thus minimizing the chance that different types of service worker behavior will be perceived by management as resistant to change.
- Goal-oriented management is tricky business, however. Because of the underlying tensions, which cannot be eliminated simply by setting goals and which cannot always be detected by monitoring, you are as apt to get it wrong as to get it right. You must also realize that "contracts" are an imperfect way of establishing goal-oriented behavior because many aspects of effective case management cannot be reduced to contractual language. You will, therefore, want to use several managerial frames in combination—symbols, sympathy, and synergy—and realize that continuous monitoring and troubleshooting are essential.

Managing Health Care

Consider two illustrations of advice to those who would reform the delivery of medical services. In a report from the Brookings Institution's Center for Public Management, John J. DiIulio, Jr., Donald F. Kettl, and Richard P. Nathan put forth "six sets of working principles to create an administratively sound national health care policy" (DiIulio et al. 1994a):

- There is no escape from administrative complexity.
- Health reform will rely on hybrid organizations.
- Before reinventing health care, rediscover the states.
- Different plans impose different management burdens.
- Define the federal and state roles.
- Stage the transition.

At the end of their paper, DiIulio, Kettl, and Nathan urge policymakers to follow four steps: define the roles; stage the tools; build the capacity; and serve the citizens. In between, the authors derive lessons from the variety of attempts to reform the health-care system. Here is an example:

Reform must build on a solid foundation, with the critical steps taken first. Those steps that cannot be achieved should not be attempted. And all of the steps have to make the system as user friendly for citizens as is possible. Careful management will minimize the transition costs.

In a related paper (1994b), these authors add to their principled approach: "Do First Things First" and "Limit Reform to the Doable."

Contrast this approach to advising public executives engaged in health-care reform with another approach with the same goal but with an altogether different intellectual agenda. Edward Lawlor (1994) proposes a framework for evaluating one of the key features of President Clinton's proposed health-care reform, Regional Health Alliances, in comparison with other institutional arrangements for financing health-care delivery:

- As risk pools
- As brokers and agents of health-care information
- As mediators of transactions costs in health care
- As procurement agencies
- As regulators of strategic behavior in the health-care market

Lawlor's implicit advice to policy executives is of a very different order than that of DiIulio, Kettl, and Nathan. Lawlor is saying, in effect: compare (i.e., ask for and study) the key institutional features of health-care reform plans together with their likely implications. In such comparative analysis, use a variety of relevant analytic lenses and frameworks; otherwise you will miss important management issues. If you follow this advice, you will discover that these plans have a complex mix of advantages and disadvantages, and you must decide which ones you care most about. Only in that way will you acquire the kind of understanding of the alternatives and their consequences that will lead to a choice that will hold up to critical scrutiny, to effective advocacy, and to purposeful management of health-care agencies.

Breaking Bureaucracy

As with the Bardach (1993) analysis discussed earlier, Barzelay starts out on an analytic path in *Breaking Through Bureaucracy* (1992). He identifies different types of accountability problems. In summarizing solutions, he says,

> Putting the new strategies into practice generally altered organizational routines in such areas as production, marketing, human resource management, financial management, executive leadership, and political oversight. In some instances, the strategies were supported by readjusting formal organizational structures and by changes in statutory authorization." (p. 94)

Barzelay also argues that

> [M]ost if not all troubles along the staff/line frontier are more likely to derive from malleable organizational cultures, constraints,

incentives, and routines than from seemingly immutable factors such as human nature or individual personality traits. In this way, deliberation can focus on solving problems rather than on lamenting conditions. [We] should be prepared to distinguish among the kinds of problems that deserve solution and to identify some concepts that can guide problem-solving efforts." (p. 91)

Later in the book, however, Barzelay reduces a complex but comprehensible argument to a set of didactic principles for managing staff agencies: (1) spread responsibility for economizing and compliance; (2) conceptualize work as providing services; (3) identify customers with care; (4) be accountable to customers; (5) reorganize to separate service from control; (6) let the customer fund the providers.

It is hard to imagine that practicing managers in various settings would be able to translate these principles into effective action. There is no apparent logic by which one proceeds from the principles to the nuanced, contingent insights in the earlier analysis. The processes by which managers can think about their work of organizational reform are not made clear. Barzelay might have summed up with proactive advice as follows: Avoid the temptation to personalize resistance to change; subordinates are probably trying to continue to do what they believe to be their jobs. Managers must work with them to redefine or restructure those jobs and must provide the incentives to do the new jobs, making sure that the reward system is well understood because it is effectively administered.

Reinventing Government
Barbara Koremenos and I (1994) analyzed a case in which the director of the Illinois Department on Aging, Victor Wirth, appeared to achieve an extraordinary success. Inheriting an agency ridden with internal conflicts and in bad repute with its contractors and constituencies, Wirth successfully refocused his department's operations on client service and on cooperation with contractors while complying with the governor's directive to cut the department's budget. This apparent demonstration that government can be better *and* cost less appears to be a classic case of "reinventing government."

"Best practice" researchers might say that Wirth transformed his agency by emphasizing customer satisfaction. His predecessor had the same emphasis, however, but could not make it operative. Other best practice researchers might argue that, unlike his predecessor, Wirth had a specific goal, and he managed by walking around and reiterating his goal until it was understood and adopted. That he did. But is having a goal and walking around all there was to transforming the agency?

Koremenos and I analyzed the data in the case using game theory as a heuristic. In our model, we identified three distinct levels of interaction within Wirth's agency, with participants in each behaving strategically, that is, choosing a strategy in light of jointly determined payoffs. In our analysis, the top two levels of the agency, Wirth and his division managers, and the division managers and their bureau chiefs, had settled down to a noncooperative equilibrium at the expense of effective service. The potential for cooperation existed at the lower, street level, where workers and clients had an ideological commitment to cooperate with each other. Such cooperation seldom occurred, however.

Our analysis revealed that the key obstacles to achieving a cooperative, client-oriented outcome for the agency as a whole were the division managers. In a series of deft moves, Wirth induced cooperation first in the field—this is what his walking around accomplished—and, finally, among the now isolated division managers. Implicitly, he figured out what he had to do to alter the strategies of his middle-level subordinates, a feat that had eluded his more conventional, compliance-oriented predecessor.

Using our analytic framework, then, we can argue that Wirth's problem was noncooperation originating at the top of the agency and institutionalized primarily at the division manager level, from where it was transmitted downward to the field. At lower levels Wirth had ideological allies whom he could easily (i.e., by walking around) mobilize to squeeze the division managers into line.

This is not a universal principle of public management, however. In a social service agency where noncooperation originates at lower levels, Wirth's walking around nattering about goals might well fail. A better strategy in such an agency might be the opposite of Wirth's: to recruit middle management to monitor the field and deliver rewards and sanctions sufficient to overcome resistance to change. What works, therefore, will depend on the internal dynamics of the agency.

Our advice to managers: when seeking to alter street-level behavior, first evaluate the incentives and beliefs motivating workers at different levels in your organization. Why do they make poor choices? Then put in place inducements that will lead workers voluntarily to choose the behavior you want.

Teaching and Learning

Reasoning that is more overtly analytical ought in principle to be more straightforward to communicate to would-be and actual practitioners than tacit, intuitive wisdom. If Barnard, Vickers, Selznick, and I are correct that effective management depends on mental discipline and skill, then those inclined toward practice ought to welcome efforts to identify and produce mastery of such skill. Success in exercises vindicating causal ordering of messy situations ought to be more satisfying than the vindication of principles that are never wrong and that leave the participant essentially unchanged.

Yet that is not the experience of a great many teachers of public management. A collective glazing over of eyes in classrooms greets professorial efforts to apply "theory." Far more welcome are trenchant, engaging stories, discussions that illustrate the uses of taxonomic ordering, and the vigorous advocacy of management principles that can be shown to have worked in practice. Exposure to colleagues with similar problems and experience with their resolution is more valued by participants in training activities than exposure to a teacher who may have little more than theory and social science data to offer.

In part, the accumulation of such experiences relates to factors not entirely flattering to either party to the transaction. Inculcating mental discipline based on conceptual heuristics requires a high order of pedagogical skill. This level of skill is achieved only after sustained trial-and-error effort; there are many bad days in learning how to be an effective teacher of practice skills. Many teachers are tempted to take paths of least resistance, either sticking with classic teaching methods and attempting to perfect them (a great lecture can be exhilarating all around), finding ways to be popular with skeptical audiences by avoiding abstractions or the intellectual challenges, or, if nothing works, abandoning altogether the effort to teach management.

For their part, many practitioners, or the inexperienced who aspire to be doers rather than thinkers, lay down a challenge to anyone daring to teach them: convince me, but I'm warning you, it won't be easy. They constitute a tough audience, at best accepting a valid challenge with a try-it-and-see attitude, at worse playing Lucy to a professorial Charlie Brown, pulling back the promise of genuine interest at every flexing of intellectual muscle. Practitioners can be rather patronizing toward those lacking the tacit understandings and insider attitudes that come from having spent time in the trenches. A display of contempt for theory may also mask insecurity or, worse, an unpleasant truth: some practitioners believe that others need to change but that they do not.

The burden of proof, of course, is on those who aspire to an analytics rather than a homiletics of managerial practice. Their challenge is to discover those pedagogical methods and materials that, when skillfully used, convince the action oriented that they will be more effective if they are thoughtful than if they are not. It will help if such convictions can be nurtured by plausible evidence that analytical practice does indeed increase the odds for success.

It will also be helpful to the cause of thoughtful management if those in the public management community more clearly identify the bases for their claims to a legitimate role in educating practitioners.

6

ART, SCIENCE, OR PROFESSION?

> If the lights that guide us ever go out, they will fade little by little,
> as if of their own accord. Confining ourselves to practice, we may
> lose sight of basic principles, and when these have been entirely
> forgotten, we may apply the methods derived from them badly; we
> might be left without the capacity to invent new methods, and
> only able to make a clumsy and an unintelligent use of wise proce-
> dures no longer understood.
>
> — Alexis de Tocqueville

Lurking in the background of debates over the relationship between public management knowledge and practice is the
subtle, infrequently acknowledged issue of the authority, jurisdiction, or professional status of the field: its power to control its
knowledge base and membership. University-based scholars and
teachers and many practitioners of public management claim, implicitly if not explicitly, to possess both uniquely valuable insights on
which to ground training and practice and legitimate authority to
graduate, certificate, or honor practitioners. The legitimacy of such
claims is challenged, however, from within and outside the university
and by factions within the public management community itself.

Establishing the legitimacy of these claims would appear to be
important to university scholars and teachers of public management.
After all, the functions of training and certification can be and often

are performed by all manner of nonuniversity entities. The old bureaus of municipal research, with their training academies, were models for such activity.[1] Today, governments, private institutes and independent academies, associations, foundations, and management consulting firms perform highly credible research, training, certification, and recognition functions. Some practitioners go so far as to argue that nonacademic actors do it with more relevance and meaning for practice than the university.

The university's claims to a special role in public management research and training are clearly justified if successful practice can be shown to require a grasp of theory and its applications and an exposure to academic experts who create the field's intellectual capital. But what of a knowledge system defined, as "best practice" teachers are inclined to do, by practice itself and therefore by whatever societal forces shape practice as comprehended not by dispassionate experts but by practitioners? If practitioners themselves insist on a self-referential view of best practice, the university's claims to an important role in scholarship and training may be exposed as little more than opportunistic entrepreneurship. The general authority —indeed, the accreditation—of the university is being invoked on behalf of commercial products—professional degrees, training programs, certificates—whose main value to practitioners is symbolic.

The controversy over the form of knowledge for practice, therefore, has significant implications for the authority, or jurisdiction, of a field's researchers, trainers, and practitioners. The interrelationships between a field's knowledge base and practice will define its jurisdiction, that is, the legitimacy and strength of its authority to define and control the knowledge and skill that certification in a professional field requires.

Knowledge and Jurisdiction

In theory, the extent to which knowledge is codified and readily ac-

---

1. The New York bureau's training academy was to become the Maxwell School of Citizenship and Public Affairs at Syracuse University.

cessible ought to have a bearing on the jurisdiction of a field and on the ease or difficulty of entering it. Figure 6.1, based on Boisot's (1986) analytic framework, illustrates the possibilities.

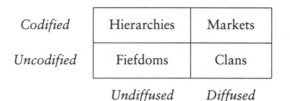

FIGURE 6.1

KNOWLEDGE AND JURISDICTION

Knowledge that is both codified and easily accessible sustains systems of impersonal exchange such as markets. Among other things, codified, diffused knowledge is the basis for the possibility of coordination among dispersed, loosely coupled actors in administrative systems. Such coordination depends on access to a commonly understood body of concepts and information. Formal and impersonal training in methods of codification, interpretation, and application prepare one to participate in markets or in administrative systems that depend on reliable, impersonal communication and coordination.

In sharp contrast, knowledge that is both uncodified and inaccessible is the foundation of fiefdoms: jurisdictions, such as movements or cults, controlled by one or only a few superior individuals. In many respects, J. Edgar Hoover's Federal Bureau of Investigation and Robert Moses's Triborough Bridge and Tunnel Authority were fiefdoms to the extent that control was highly personalized, unreviewable, and unappealable. The elect participate in fiefdoms. There is no formal training for acquiring the cachet that enabled Hoover and Moses to manage as they did.[2]

2. Leonard White (1936) was critical of the principles of such great figures as Richelieu, Burke, Hamilton, and Lord Haldane: "Theirs was . . .

Codified knowledge whose accessibility is restricted to authorized individuals such as employees of an agency is the foundation for bureaucracy, a regime of rules and structures defining and restricting exchange among employees and between employees and the outside world. To perform and manage, one must "learn the agency." Uncodified or tacit knowledge that is diffused among numerous individuals who share a system of values or beliefs or conventions is the basis for what Ouchi (1980) termed clans. In clans, performance ambiguity is high but proper socialization ensures trust, cooperation, and the disinclination to deviate or defect; clans tend to be self-regulating. One can prepare for managing in a clan environment by study, but socialization and apprenticeship on the job would appear much more essential.[3]

In a related vein, Bozeman (1993) has proposed "a typology of knowledge in public-private management." "Ordinary knowledge," he says, comprises varieties of anecdotal evidence, conventional wisdom, and "institutionally embedded knowledge." Those who possess this type of uncodified but partially diffused knowledge resemble Boisot/Ouchi clans: communities united by a sharing of "thick social understandings" or a common culture. "Wisdom," according to Bozeman, comprises a variety of subcategories of knowledge accessible as literature where acceptance or learning depends on "intersubjective validation." Regimes in which control is based on a leader's wisdom resemble Boisot's fiefs, in which authority is exercised by a guru or gifted leader whose appeal to believers is essentially intersubjective. "Theory-seeking literature," in Bozeman's view, comprises familiar forms of academic knowledge and, presumably, other analytic knowledge, whether embedded in an institution such as a public agency or an academic discipline or widely and impersonally available, perhaps in published form, to those with the requisite intellectual skill.

This kind of analysis brings us quite naturally to the question of whether or not the claimants to authority on any of these bases—

---

essentially a personal divination, an intuition certainly not shared by all and not understood by many" (p. 21).

3. An application of this kind of argument is in DiIulio (1994).

codified, analytic knowledge, insider familiarity, or superior wisdom—can be said to constitute not only a community of interest and social control but a profession. Theory suggests that claims to professional status must be specifically justified. In Eliot Friedson's view,

> "Profession" is synonymous with "occupation": it refers to specialized work by which one gains a living in an exchange economy. But it is not just *any* kind of work that professionals do. The kind of work they do is esoteric, complex, and discretionary in character: it requires theoretical knowledge, skill, and judgment that ordinary people do not possess, may not wholly comprehend, and cannot readily evaluate. (Friedson 1994, 200)

Abbott (1988) adds the useful insight that the system of professions can be broadly understood in terms of a vacancy model, that is, categories of positions to be filled and the basis for entry into and mobility within such categories. Thus a profession is founded on theory-grounded knowledge and formal opportunities to use it with the possibility of ascending to higher levels of responsibility and reward.

Profession means more than expert knowledge and occupational affiliation, however. Friedson further identifies a profession as an "organized autonomy." The professional "is self-directing in his work" (1974, 431). Autonomy is achieved when "[a profession] has obtained a legal or political position of privilege that protects it from encroachment by other professions"; a profession controls "the production and particularly the application of knowledge and skill to the work it performs." Again, Abbott adds the important insight that "only a knowledge system governed by abstractions can redefine its problems and tasks, defend them from interlopers, and seize new problems.... Abstraction enables survival in the competitive system of professions" (1988, 8). In other words, the requirement for successful mastery of essential abstractions constitutes a powerful basis for professional autonomy.

A requirement that entrants must submit to extended training in a segregated professional program in order to achieve the necessary mastery of abstract concepts and their application can be a useful way of establishing autonomy. Abstractions are the province of the academy. Thus, to complete the syllogism, a profession that requires a mastery of abstract reasoning and seeks to restrict entry on the basis of its mastery will find a natural home in the university, the only social institution expected to be fully engaged in abstract learning.[4]

Finally, Friedson notes that professional dominance, for example, that of medicine, can serve the same functions and look the same to clients or outsiders as bureaucracy, in that outsiders are confronted with a regime of formal rules and procedures. What, then, if the would-be profession is bureaucracy itself? How does one distinguish bureaucracy as a means, chosen by experts to serve professional objectives, and bureaucracy as an end in itself, that is, a self-perpetuating creation of special, but not necessarily professional, interests?

A helpful answer to this question is provided by James Q. Wilson (1989), who argues that "because the behavior of a professional is not entirely shaped by organizational incentives, the way such a person defines his or her task may reflect more the standards of the external reference group than the preferences of the internal management" (p. 60). Certification by the academy and continuing association with a university-certified group is a basis for the professional status of an occupational category comprising public officials. Employment by government does not automatically confer professional status; one must be suitably credentialed by external authority.[5]

Applying this reasoning, the public management community, including both its public administration and public policy provinces, is

4. Friedson notes that there is autonomy by default—the public doesn't care and won't encroach—and claims to autonomy by "professions"—for example, social workers, schoolteachers—which aren't really dominant and for which there is no "hierarchy of institutionalized expertise" (1994, 434).

5. In a similar attempt to separate public employment from professional status, social workers have drawn a distinction between those with a social work credential and those government employees who are correctly identified as case workers, not social workers. Elementary and secondary school teachers have had even more trouble establishing their authority in their credentials rather than their jobs.

confronted with questions: (1) Is there an "occupation of public management"? (2) If not—or if the answer is ambiguous—must any claim that public management is a profession be rejected? Is public management, instead, a craft guild or, of even less stature, merely a kind of job or task ordering? (3) Does the knowledge base of practice necessarily include theory, thus justifying a university affiliation as an essential component of authority, legitimacy, or, even in the absence of occupational affiliation, professional identity?

A common objective of those within the public management community has been the creation of an external reference community for public managers, for example, Kelman's invisible "public management culture" or visible membership in the National Academy of Public Administration, linking practitioners, scholars, and teachers. The question raised here is whether such an external reference community constitutes a profession. Residents of the public administration province may have little trouble with the answer: we have our occupation, we have our theory, we have our textbooks, we have our credentials, and we have our autonomy (i.e., values that transcend jobs). The issue for public policy schools is whether a community of interest created without an occupation as foundation can be a profession or is, instead, a craft guild or even a club? The issue raised by recent controversies over the "best practice" approach to knowledge is whether the university can claim to have an essential, as opposed to an opportunistic, role in training practitioners.

Public Administration as Occupation

With the advent of modern bureaucratic government was born a new occupational category: the formally qualified and tenured civil servant. This occupation was to provide the foundation for the emergence of specialized study in and training for the new field of public administration. The civic reformers responsible for this achievement were themselves from emerging social elites in business, law, and other specialized fields. Their goal was expert administration of the public's increasingly consequential business by officials selected for their skills and ability rather than for political loyalty (Skowronek 1982, 54–55).

To justify claims to conferring professional status, in the manner of law and medicine, the study and practice of public administration would require two things: (1) a knowledge base, that is, a body of theory, concepts, and wisdom that could be applied to problems arising in practice and that could form the basis for preprofessional training; and (2) jurisdiction, that is, a link between the training of experts and their performance of their work sufficiently demonstrable to withstand competition from other professions or from nonprofessionals, enabling these new experts to control their domain.

As suggested earlier, there is nothing inevitable linking the growth of professionalism to universities; it was not so in England and not so in early American training for public administration and social work. That the two have become linked in America results in part from historical accident: concurrent developments in the professions and in the evolution of American universities. Abbott (1988) notes that

> the new university took shape just as the American professions were recovering from the Jacksonian era, whose democratization had overthrown institutions of professional control. . . . Thus while in fact professional education by no means required university affiliation . . . profession after profession turned to the university for help in seizing control of its own educational apparatus. (p. 207)

But unlike the unified German university after which American research universities were modeled, professional schools "were in the [American] university but not of it. . . . The professors remained professionals first and professors second." Thus, Abbott argues, the American university became a holding company for autonomous and competitive faculties, some wholly dedicated to the scholarly mission of the university, others finding it expedient to use the university as a base for various externally oriented activities.

From their university base, academics such as Woodrow Wilson, Frank Goodnow, and Leonard D. White, drawing on European antecedents, initiated a literature of ideas concerning the practice of public administration (Bozeman 1979). But the main boost to professionalism came with the forging of a link to what was then held to be science. Formal theoretical foundations for administrative practice were adapted from the immensely influential studies of Frederick Taylor (1911). Formulating a "science of administration" became the goal of the growing body of public administration scholars in American universities and municipal research bureaus.

The central idea informing the creation of this "scientific" knowledge base was that politics and administration are separable domains. Luther Gulick argued that

> more programs can be brought about in government through an application of the scientific spirit, through impartial research, through the testing of ideas, and the discovery of principles of administration than through any program of political reform which mankind has yet adopted. (1928, 102)

Appropriating the ideas of scientific management, public administration's leading scholars formulated a set of canonical "scientific" principles and structural precepts that ought to govern all administrative activity. In fairly short order, as Bozeman (1979, 34) puts it, "leading public administrationists had the ear and the confidence of presidents, governors, and mayors. The golden age of public administration had arrived."

The structural/functional orientation of the emerging knowledge base of public administration led quite naturally to the steady emergence of circumscribed subfields and specialized knowledge based on particular occupational classifications. Thus "city management" became a recognized and relatively secure professional subfield, as did public budgeting and, later, personnel administration and program evaluation, each with its own knowledge base and membership organizations.

The golden age of intellectual hegemony was to end rather abruptly, for a simple reason. The profession's founding idea could not withstand either intellectual scrutiny or the testimony of experience. In 1940, Carl J. Friedrich argued that "public policy, to put it flatly, is a continuous process, the formation of which is inseparable from its execution" (Friedrich 1940, 6). In the immediate postwar years, a new generation of public administration scholars, many with experience in New Deal and wartime public administration, demolished the notion that administration could be governed by canonical principles. Further, such scholars suggested that several fields of academic inquiry emerging outside public administration's domain had a direct bearing on public administration scholarship and training (Simon 1976; Simon, Smithburg, and Thompson 1950).

Recognition of the inseparability of administrative and political domains and of the universality of administration could hardly have left the relatively young profession of public administration unchanged. The study of governance was thrown wide open to incursions from a number of competing intellectual domains, and a once robust canonical orthodoxy rather quickly degenerated into an unruly heterodoxy. If public administration were to withstand threats to its jurisdiction in the face of these incursions, the new fields of study would have to be incorporated into public administration training. To the extent that the profession was lax or incompetent in applying promising new bodies of abstract knowledge to the problems in its domain, it would be vulnerable to challenge and perhaps even disappear.

Public administration was unquestionably weakened when a preoccupation with practice allowed more basic inquiry to find its home in political science (Bendor 1994). A more serious threat seemed to have materialized with the noisy birth of graduate public policy schools, which arrogantly claimed to be taking over the more glamorous assignments in policy execution. Traditional public administration, its own weakly defined jurisdiction challenged both intellectually and by competitors for its students and for the loyalties of its alumni, became even more confused.

Some public administrationists sought refuge in the profession's traditional occupational orientation toward the tenured civil service. The more ambitious of them embraced the creation in 1978 of the federal Senior Executive Service to redefine and extend public administration's professional jurisdiction into the higher reaches of governance. Others sought to reorganize public administration's jurisdiction around normative propositions and value orientations that the positivistic policy schools and disciplines disdained. Still others, recognizing the importance of a relatively secure organizational base for the conduct of professional education and research, sought to redefine the intellectual challenge of schools of public policy in a broader organizational context. They began importing useful intellectual developments in the social sciences on behalf of public administration's own broadened concept of public management.

It is a debate that continues. To John Rohr (1986), the issue is the legitimation of "the expert agency tasked with important governing functions through loosely drawn statutes that empower unelected officials to undertake ... important matters ..." (p. xi). The professional goal must be to sustain "the integrity of the Public Administration as an institution of government" (p. ix). H. George Frederickson (1994, 2) proposes to broaden the domain of public administration "to include the administrative or implementation aspects of all forms and manifestations of collective public activity." In other words, "public" administration is not just "government" administration.

Frederickson also advocates a special sensitivity "to the distinctions between the roles of those who are elected and those who are civil servants" (1994, 5). He would not intrude on the policymakers' terrain: the role of public administration is to push "political masters," by which he means elected officials and their assistants—the policymakers—to face up to policy dilemmas that make good management impossible: contradictory policy, incoherent policy, intentionally vague policy. Implicitly, Frederickson seems to be arguing that working on behalf of manageable policy might well be the proper mission of public administration's sister public policy schools.

A different kind of response to the challenges facing the profession arises from more academic concerns. A common complaint within public administration is the fragmentation of the field's intellectual domain among subfields in political science, in other social sciences, and in the applied scholarship of professional schools. Particular targets of criticism are researchers employing "rational actor" theory and other concepts associated with positive political economy, whose rigor is seductive to ambitious scholars if not to practicing administrators. There are those, such as Kenneth Meier (1993), who decisively reject "invasions" from adjacent disciplines as corrupting and argue for a pure form of theory within public administration.

In combination, these various responses have ensured that public administration as a profession, while weakened, has not become moribund. One reason for its survival is the fact that tenured civil servants continue to constitute a distinct and significant occupational category in American life. If the founding premise that policy and administration are inseparable has lost all intellectual credibility, the premise nonetheless survives as a myth sustaining claims to independence by career civil servants. As long as the protective myth is strong, the challenge of redefining the expertise and jurisdiction of public administration as a profession is all the more interesting. No longer a mere technocrat executing mandates written by others, the professional civil servant, at both lower and higher levels of responsibility, openly participates in the democratic process of policy formation. The 1990s fascination with "reinventing government" reinforced many civil servants' sense of their importance.

A second reason for the survival of public administration as a profession is the fact that, whether separable from politics or not, the concept of administration as a human activity lends itself to a high order of abstraction. Simon, Thompson, and Smithburg (1991, 4, 6), for example, defined administration as "cooperative group behavior.... [Thus] any person engaged in an activity in cooperation with other persons is engaged in administration." Frederickson refers to "collective" action, a defining concept with strong theoretical implications. If, as noted earlier, abstraction is essential to competitive success in the system of professions, public administration is still in the competition.

The appeal of reductive abstractions creates a tension within public administration, however. Use of abstractions sustains the claim that entry into public administration occupations requires university-based preparation of a distinctive kind. But it requires scholars and teachers to remain fully interdisciplinary, a challenge of increasing difficulty as the disciplines evolve and become more diverse and abstract themselves. Further, grounding in abstract reasoning is alienating to some in both the academy and the practice community.

It is forgivable if public administrationists appear to weave uncertainly as they seek to reconcile these tensions.

Public Policy as Craft Guild

It was in the context of public administration's heterodox confusion that the challenge to the jurisdiction of public administration from the public policy schools arose. In the late 1960s, a new form of professional education for public service began to emerge: the graduate school of public policy. This development was the coming to fruition of a notion, analysis for executive decision making, whose antecedents are several: the New Deal concepts of a brain trust to support national leaders and of comprehensive planning and analysis as a basis for social mobilization and public policy; successful applications of mathematical modeling and statistical methods to operations planning during World War II; and postwar applications of economics and other social science disciplines to problems of national resource allocation, initially in the area of national security but rapidly if not convincingly spreading to most domains of public concern.

In contrast to public administration's focus on the functions and values of the permanent government, teachers and scholars in the public policy community have chosen to concentrate on the contributions to public policy achievement of a transitory cast of executives and their assistants who hold high-level appointments for limited periods and are usually drawn largely from other professions: law, politics, business, and academia. The intellectual task facing these teachers and scholars is to demonstrate, because it cannot be assumed, that specialized knowledge and skill beyond those already possessed by appointees are needed to perform these transitory public executive roles.

The implicit claim of the new schools was that the most effective leverage over public policy achievement is exercised by elected and appointed executives and their immediate, noncareer subordinates, who have specialized intellectual preparation. Abbott (1988) has argued that professions acquire the status of their clients. In effect, the new schools sought to hive off for their special form of training individuals aspiring to high if impermanent status in government, leaving aspirants to lower-status careers to the traditional schools of public administration.

Questions of career progression were bound to arise among the ambitious students in these new schools. They wanted to know what fate awaited them, the nature of life after serving as a special assistant to a cabinet officer or as a policy analyst in a creative period of policy change. Whereas public administration could answer its students' questions by reference to the classical vacancy model, public policy had to invent career scenarios for the public policy graduate. It was surmised that graduates would move in and out of particular governmental positions, perhaps to the private corporate or management consulting sectors, perhaps to the nonprofit sector or think tanks, perhaps from one level of government to another. More recently, public policy schools have been placing their graduates directly into the private sector, disproving the notion that policy analysis skills are marketable only to governments. Through bobbing and weaving, public policy graduates would presumably ascend to higher levels of pay and responsibility, eventually, perhaps, becoming senior political appointees, elected officials, or successful entrepreneurs.

Reinforcing their bid for high status, these emerging professional schools of public policy sought to found their domain on the abstract systems of knowledge that had become immensely popular in the social science disciplines, especially economics. The new schools did not directly challenge the occupationally based domain of public administration and its concern for officeholding. Instead, their founders sought to establish their version of education for government on intellectual performance using the technical skill of policy analysis. Faculty were initially drawn primarily from the social science disciplines, and their intellectual aspirations mimicked the standards of the disciplines.[6] Don K. Price, the Kennedy School's founding dean, put the matter succinctly:

> Universities, in the main, cannot do the job of conducting the more immediately practical types of training as well as the government

6. To this day, tenure in most public policy schools usually depends on at least the approbation of local leaders in the relevant disciplines.

agencies can.... [T]heir essential contribution ... should be to make the best use of their institutional skills and habits, which commit them to a more fundamental and indeed theoretical approach, at both the preentry and midcareer levels of education for public service. (1975, 250)

Almost immediately, however, jurisdictional tensions arose within the new policy schools. They have come to have various axes: analysis versus politics; an identification with economics or other quantitative disciplines versus an identification with political science; a technical, program/task focus versus a strategic, leadership-oriented focus; and, finally, traditional teaching—lectures, problem sets, tests—versus teaching via the case method, workshops, internships, and other forms of experiential activity. Public management teachers and scholars more or less sought to establish intellectual distance not only from traditional political science and public administration but from their more formally analytical and dispassionate colleagues. A recent complaint by Martin Levin and Mary Bryna Sanger is revealing of the tensions: "Public policy programs have not as yet taken the reins away from the policy-analytical economists in order to emphasize and celebrate the importance of public management" (Levin and Sanger 1994, 306).

As the remark by Levin and Sanger implies, the issues are as much jurisdictional as intellectual.[7] The field of public management as it began to emerge in the new graduate programs in public policy sought to provide normative justification for and prescriptive guidance to the work of public managers even as their forebears in public administration had done in their "golden age." An academic com-

7. An additional clue to the existence of jurisdictional tensions is the disinclination of public management faculty at the Kennedy School to include Harvard scholars such as Edwin Banfield, Arthur Maass, James Q. Wilson (and even Michel Crozier when he was in residence at Harvard) in their intellectual community. Even the distinguished Don K. Price, with his priceless background in public administration, seemed to be an outsider in the school of which he was founding dean. Boundaries at other policy schools are more blurred.

munity that scoffed at the old-fashioned POSDCORB began generating its own lists of canonical principles of management and continues to do so, their formulators—unfazed by the ghost of Herbert Simon and his withering scorn—seemingly yearning for a special niche and status even as Peters and Waterman found theirs.

Another development in the evolving schools of public policy was even more consequential. After only little more than a decade of concentration on precareer education of putative policymakers, these schools, and especially scholars and teachers identified with public management, sought to extend their jurisdiction by establishing certificated executive development programs for both career and appointed officials at the most senior levels of federal, state, and local governments. Though perhaps possessing other professional degrees, participants in the new executive programs would be trained in the higher-order mental, behavioral, and leadership skills and values associated with effective executive performance in the public domain.

By enlarging the public policy schools' domain to include executive education, for which high-status business schools were the model, public management faculty also strengthened their claim over resources for knowledge development and for the particular forms of knowledge that were thought most suitable for executive education. These favored forms, many of which are depicted in some detail by Barzelay (1993), have come to be known as "best practice research" in the light of their ethnographic/experiential emphasis.

Viewed in the historical context of how professions evolve, this evolution of the public management subfield within public policy schools may seem curious. The consolidation of a profession's jurisdiction ordinarily occurs through the evolution of its knowledge base toward higher levels of intellectual abstraction, thus raising the costs of entry to the profession's practice domain by would-be competitors. The necessity to master arcane knowledge for specialized responsibilities justifies and reinforces the need for and effectiveness of more formal barriers to entry such as ethics codes, licensure, accreditation, board examinations, and certification.

Advocates of "best practice" knowledge, in contrast, seem to be depending on an uncodified but richly textured folk wisdom and craft techniques reinforced by elite certification to sustain their jurisdiction against competitors from law, business, the social sciences, public administration, and, uncomfortably nearby, policy analysis, with its economistic orientation. This evolution is justified by those who have led it as fulfilling the profession's original mission of informing practice—by training entry-level professionals, by offering mid-career and executive training to practitioners, and by offering advice and, increasingly, inspiration and encouragement to all. The urge to establish a protected domain within public policy, impenetrable by economists and other social scientists, for jurisdictional rather than intellectual reasons, is an important part of the explanation.

Jurisdictional issues have, however, with the occasional exception of the Levin and Sanger remark, been implicit in professional discourse within the field of public policy. Self-conscious use of the term "profession" is hardly ever associated with the term "public management." Issues of jurisdiction are nonetheless present. A general goal of the public management community is exceptional competence in managing the public's business. How can political appointees can be persuaded to aspire to greater competence and to identify themselves as participants in a public management culture? Are there particular types of executive failures that the public management community cannot condone? Is there such a thing as public executive malpractice? These are questions ultimately bearing on the question of "professionalism."

The issue of authority is largely unacknowledged in part because the ideological slant of the "best practice" movement discourages it. Claims to specialized knowledge go against the democratic grain of lay entry and accountability to publics.[8] Best practice implies that there are no experts, little specialized knowledge, and few learned skills involved in effective public management. Instead, there are effective artisans of practice, whose success is as much a reflection of character as of knowledge. The academy's role is to appreci-

8. It is ironic that in their suspicion of technical expertise, "best practice" proponents echo the earlier arguments of Lasswell, Dror, and others associated with the "policy sciences" who were and continue to be opponents of elite-dominated, top-down rationality.

ate them and to have the good sense to provide them with an imprimatur, with an audience among the aspiring, and with opportunities to talk among themselves.

While entrepreneurial motivations undoubtedly explain some of this evolution in public management, there is, I believe, a deeper reason. Protestations to the contrary, authority is to be sustained, not by codified expertise and communicable mastery of abstract ideas, but by the appeal of membership in an elite subculture or clan whose members are bound together by shared experiences (degree or training programs), rituals (case discussions), and symbols (of which university affiliation, attested to by certificates and logo'ed T-shirts, is among the most valued). Despite their democratic pretensions, advocates of best practice may be creating, inadvertently to be sure, a mandarinate anointed but not trained by the university, men and women entitled to deference and respect for having been recognized by a great academy of disinterested learning.

Public Management: Community or Profession?

Public management within its two provinces will continue to be shaped by the missions of the schools. Public administration programs, for example, have the responsibility to prepare students for entry-level career positions, primarily (because that's where the jobs are) in state and local governments. It will be surprising if the concerns of scholars do not continue to emphasize what I have called the ground of government: structures and functions, administrative routines, the values of public service, and the diversity of skills needed for career development.

Within public administration, public management defined as the executive function in government will be carried by the strong currents within public administration as a whole. Figures, that is, executives as biographically specific actors, will seldom be allowed to stand out from their institutional backgrounds.[9] This inclination on the part of public administrationists to stay grounded should be ben-

9. Rainey (1991) puts a characteristic spin on the subject: "organizations need effective management."

eficial for public management scholarship and training. They will necessarily keep the subject connected to deeper structural and behavioral issues, counteracting the often superficial elitism of public policy's influential homiletic school.

A strong intellectual influence will depend, however, on the field's retaining and strengthening its affinities with academic disciplines and adjacent fields of inquiry (Bendor 1994; Moe 1994). Should the field succumb to the urging of some that public administration go it alone intellectually or become preachers of a civic religion, then contributions to an analytics of public management will be few.

Public management scholarship originating in the public policy community will also continue to be shaped by the missions of the schools: the education and training of executive and civil servant elites. Not surprisingly, the scholarly values manifest in the literature have changed over time as the mission of the public policy schools has broadened from an initial emphasis on providing precareer training to include educating and providing learning opportunities for numerous audiences, including practitioners performing different governmental, or even nongovernmental, roles and in various stages of their careers.

Thus public policy's initial emphasis on contributions that balance art and science on behalf of goals that were primarily intellectual has given way to an emphasis on contributions that are, to borrow Riker's term, more heresthetic,[10] that resonate with life as practitioners experience it, and that serve the goals of experiential reflection and societal reform.

This is an oversimplification, of course. The public policy community is attractive to management-oriented scholars who, without necessarily abandoning their disciplinary affiliations, enjoy submitting their contributions to a more intellectually tolerant, problem-oriented, and worldly audience. The public management milieu within the public policy community affects intellectual commerce

10. Heresthetics is defined as an art that "involves the use of language to accomplish some purpose: to arrive at truth, to communicate, to persuade, and to manipulate" (Riker 1986, x). Cf. Reich (1988).

with academic communities in several other ways that are costly in terms of intellectual authority, however.

First, the more promising, specifically intellectual innovations originating within the public policy community are, as suggested in chapter 2, more likely to be honored abroad than at home. Allison's seminal work continues to be generative within political science (Bendor and Hammond 1989, 1992), as is the work of Pressman and Wildavsky and Bardach within public administration, long after they have largely been retired as seminal figures by the public policy community. A great many of the most popular contributions in public management now have a *sui generis* quality, and one must search outside the community to discover whether they are having a wider intellectual impact.

Second, within public policy, academic literatures are valued less as sources of theories and methods to discipline observation and analysis and more as sources of symbolic vocabulary useful in conveying an impression of learnedness. Public management scholars within the public policy community have little intrinsic intellectual need for one another or, for that matter, for colleagues in other disciplines. Well-defined intellectual frontiers do not emerge from the cumulative results of scholarship, and there are virtually no specifically academic disputes. As a result, principles proliferate; rules are few and tenuous.[11]

Third, scholars of organizations and institutions who are interested in addressing academic problems are not likely to feel strong attractions to what they see as the largely atheoretical public management milieu within the public policy community. Law and busi-

---

11. A symposium on whether participation in work and training should be voluntary or mandatory for work recipients produced, instead of rules and their application, "policy arguments that are persuasive to the extent that they are well motivated, carefully crafted from available analytic and empirical materials, and accessible to thoughtful readers.... Dispassionate readers are likely to react as much to the authors' scrupulousness and craftsmanship, to the cogency and apparent relevance of their insights and judgments, as to their reliance on formal models, rigorous empirical research, and citations from the literature" (Lynn 1989, 305–6).

ness schools, for example, have attracted social scientists to their faculties to collaborate in important intellectual developments—for example, in finance, law and economics, regulation, and agency theory—viewed as outside the purview of the disciplines themselves. These bodies of theory have proved in turn to have considerable practical value. Within public administration, highly codified and well-respected subfields such as public budgeting have emerged. Subfields such as program evaluation and nonprofit organizations are only weakly rooted in public policy programs.

No such developments have originated in public policy schools. Only two important textbooks in its specialty, policy analysis (Stokey and Zeckhauser 1978; Weimer and Vining 1989), have been produced by public policy scholars, and both have been largely derivative of ideas in the social sciences. The fast pace set by early public management scholarship has not been sustained. Other than to add sinew to the methodological bones of policy analysis, detours into social science have been regarded as a distraction and as having excessive opportunity costs in forfeited attention of practitioners.

A Duty to Reflect

To the extent that these characterizations are accurate, they are not necessarily to be either deplored or celebrated. But surely reflection is in order. Richard Elmore has argued that "public policy programs originated from a self-conscious attempt to reconstitute the intellectual foundations of *professional* education for the public service by introducing greater conceptual clarity to the field and by focusing more attention on developing the analytic competencies of students" (Elmore 1991, 168; italics added).

Was this overarching goal appropriate to begin with? Has the goal changed, and do different standards of intellectual performance now apply? If so, why? Have Schon and Rein (1994) and Barzelay (1993) supplanted Allison, Bardach, and Elmore in defining the appropriate directions for public management scholarship?[12] Are Lind-

12. It is interesting to compare advice to public administrationists by Bendor (1994) and Moe (1994), emphasizing applied heuristics, with ad-

blom (1989) and Reich (1990) defining the new directions for practice?

A field with little evident interest in evaluating "competing explanations" for phenomena or in avoiding "selection bias" in assembling evidence for arguments or in protecting against "ex post theorizing" cannot claim that it is bringing conceptual clarity to the executive function in government or developing the analytic skills needed for thoughtful practice (Overman and Boyd 1994).

Not having to be bound by conventional academic standards of intellectual merit was, of course, a goal of many of the founders of the public policy schools. By shaking off "the dead hand of social science," as one of the field's mentors put it, the schools' faculties could pursue a deeper, more socially significant, and more resonant truth. The problem with such academic freedom is that it may be difficult to discern if there are any standards at all (Overman 1994; Schon and Rein 1994).

For all the principles of intellectual probity one might invoke to justify university programs, however, highly practical considerations influence the content and directions of public management scholarship, particularly in the public policy community. The fact that there are relatively few teachers, courses, doctoral students, and research grants in public management precludes much depth or diversity of scholarship in the conventional academic sense. Except in programs maintaining close relations with the disciplines, moreover, there seem to be few if any incentives to seek the intellectual approval of academic peers inside, and especially outside, the community. As a result, noncumulative, *sui generis* contributions proliferate.

This situation poses a problem. In a field relieved of the mandate to engage in empirical validation in any scientific sense—and having no theory-building traditions of its own analogous to those of either the disciplines or the well-established professions—it is dif-

---

vice to the public policy community by Schon and Rein (1994, esp. 203–9), emphasizing frame reflection. If such advice is heeded, the two communities will be pulled in opposite directions, though not in directions inappropriate to their missions.

ficult to establish meaningful intellectual communication, much less maintain relationships with adjacent fields that do have standards for evaluating the validity of statements. Propositions derived from a biased selection of case materials cannot be compared or meaningfully evaluated. Statements that are "always true" do not tend to stimulate critical inquiry. An argument that "my principle is more universal, deep, timeless, and powerful than yours" is unlikely to generate much intellectual excitement.

Creating a repertoire of abstractions and engaging in empirical validation of predictions, conjectures, and statements is central to any scholarly activity directed at professional performance, where scholarship refers to a process of "grasping the truth amid appearances."[13] Public management scholars who share this belief will seek to discover "rules," and, moreover, rules of a more than trivial or obvious character, rather than merely add to the already long list of putative principles by canvassing yet another cohort of compliant practitioners for pearls of reflective wisdom. An intellectual field cannot be built on self reports by the subjects of interest.

Embracing the concept of analytic practice would help dispel the isolation of public management scholars within the public policy community from other academic communities, including public administration. It would increase the possibility of the public policy community's making serious contributions to theory, for example, of bureaucratic autonomy; executive discretion and accountability; results-oriented institutional design; the relationships among politics, management, organizations, and service delivery; and manageable public policy.

It would serve an even more important purpose. By demonstrating that intellectual skill is a defining feature of effective public management, scholars and teachers of thoughtful practice might rescue university professional programs from the taint of commercialism. They would thus enhance the university's authority, and by implication their own authority, not only in a professional but in a moral sense. Where else but in university programs in public management

13. The phrase is from Hudson and Jacot (1991, 14).

can society turn for sustained commitment to a morally responsible statecraft based on the authority of intellectual integrity in public life?

REFERENCES

ABBOTT, ANDREW
1988   *The System of Professions: An Essay on the Division of Expert Labor.* Chicago: University of Chicago Press.

ALLISON, GRAHAM T., JR.
1971   *Essence of Decision: Explaining the Cuban Missile Crisis.* Boston: Little, Brown.
1979   "Public Management: Are They Fundamentally Alike in All Unimportant Respects?" In *Proceedings for the Public Management Research Conference,* 19–20 November. Washington, D.C.: Office of Personnel Management. OPM Document 127-53-1:27–38.

ALLISON, GRAHAM, AND PETER SZANTON
1976   *Remaking Foreign Policy: The Organizational Connection.* New York: Basic Books.

ALTSHULER, ALAN A.
1988   "A Comment on Groping Along." *Journal of Policy Analysis and Management* 7:4:664–67.

ARROW, KENNETH J.
1985   "The Economics of Agency." In *Principals and Agents: The Structure of Business,* ed. John W. Pratt and Richard J. Zeckhauser, 37–51. Boston: Harvard Business School.

BARDACH, EUGENE
1972   *The Skill Factor in Politics: Repealing the Mental Commitment Laws in California.* Berkeley: University of California Press.

1977   *The Implementation Game: What Happens After a Bill Becomes Law.* Cambridge: MIT Press.

1984   "Public Management—The Pedagogical Challenge." In *Teaching Public Management,* Proceedings of a Workshop to Assess Materials and Strategies for Teaching Public Management, Seattle, 9–11 May, 13–55.

1987   "From Practitioner Wisdom to Scholarly Knowledge and Back Again." *Journal of Policy Analysis and Management* 7:1:188–99.

1993   *Improving the Productivity of JOBS Programs.* New York: Manpower Demonstration Research Corporation.

BARDACH, EUGENE, AND ROBERT A. KAGAN

1982   *Going by the Book: The Problem of Regulatory Unreasonableness.* Philadelphia: Temple University Press.

BARNARD, CHESTER I.

1968   *The Functions of the Executive.* 30th anniversary ed. Cambridge: Harvard University Press, 301–22.

BARZELAY, MICHAEL

1992a   *Breaking through Bureaucracy: A New Vision for Managing in Government.* Berkeley: University of California Press.

1992b   "Origins and Development of Public Management." Course Syllabus, John F. Kennedy School of Government, Harvard University, Spring.

1993   "The Single Case Study as Intellectually Ambitious Inquiry." *Journal of Public Administration Research and Theory* 3:3:305–18.

BEHN, ROBERT D.

1988   "Management by Groping Along." *Journal of Policy Analysis and Management* 8:3:643–63.

1991a   "Homestead Air Force Base." A Teaching Case plus Sequel. Institute of Policy Sciences, Duke University.

1991b   *Leadership Counts: Lessons for Public Managers from the Massachusetts Welfare, Training, and Employment Program.* Cambridge: Harvard University Press.

1992   "Baseball Management and Public Management: The Testable vs. the Important." *Journal of Policy Analysis and Management* 11:2:315–21.

1993   "Case Analysis Research and Managerial Effectiveness: Learning How to Lead Organizations Up Sand Dunes." In Bozeman (1993, 40–54).

BENDOR, JONATHAN

1990   "Formal Models of Bureaucracy: A Review." In Lynn and Wildavsky (1990, 373–417).

1994   "The Fields of Bureaucracy and Public Administration: Basic and Applied Research." *Journal of Public Administration Research and Theory* 4:1:27–39.

BENDOR, JONATHAN, AND THOMAS H. HAMMOND

1989   "Rethinking Allison's Models." Prepared for presentation at the annual meeting of the American Political Science Association, Atlanta, 31 August–3 September.

1992   "Rethinking Allison's Models." *American Political Science Review* 86:2:301–22.

BERNSTEIN, MARVER H.

1958   *The Job of the Federal Executive.* Washington, D.C.: Brookings Institution.

BOISOT, MAX H.

1986   "Markets and Hierarchies in a Cultural Perspective." *Organization Studies* 7:2:137–60.

BOLMAN, LEE G., AND TERRENCE E. DEAL

1991   *Reframing Organizations: Artistry, Choice, and Leadership.* San Francisco: Jossey-Bass.

BOWER, JOSEPH L.

1977   "Effective Public Management." *Harvard Business Review* 55:2:131–40.

1983   *The Two Faces of Management: An American Approach to Leadership in Business and Politics.* Boston: Houghton Mifflin.

BOWER, JOSEPH L., AND CHARLES J. CHRISTENSON

1978   *Public Management: Text and Cases.* Homewood, Ill.: Richard D. Irwin.

BOZEMAN, BARRY

1979   *Public Management and Policy Analysis.* New York: St. Martin's Press.

1993   "Theory, 'Wisdom,' and the Character of Knowledge in

Public Management: A Critical View of the Theory-Practice Linkage." In *Public Management: The State of the Art,* ed. Barry Bozeman, 27–39. San Francisco: Jossey-Bass.

BOZEMAN, BARRY, AND JEFFREY D. STRAUSSMAN
1990   *Public Management Strategies: Guidelines for Managerial Effectiveness.* San Francisco: Jossey-Bass.

BRINTON, J.Y.
1913   "Some Powers and Problems of the Federal Administration." 62d Cong., 2d sess. Senate Document 1054. Quoted in Short (1923, 23).

BRODKIN, EVELYN Z.
1986   *The False Promise of Administrative Reform: Implementing Quality Control in Welfare.* Philadelphia: Temple University Press.
1987   "Policy Politics: If We Can't Govern, Can We Manage?" *Political Science Quarterly* 102:4:571–87.
1990   "Implementation as Policy Politics." In *Implementation and the Public Policy Process: Opening Up the Black Box,* ed. D. Palumbo and D. Calista. Westport, Conn.: Greenwood Press.
1992   "Teenage Pregnancy and the Dilemma of Social Policymaking." *Early Parenthood and Coming of Age in the 1990s,* ed. Margaret K. Rosenheim and Mark F. Testa. New Brunswick, N.J.: Rutgers University Press.

BROUDY, H.
1981   *Truth and Credibility: The Citizen's Dilemma.* New York: Longman.

BURNHAM, JAMES
1941   *The Managerial Revolution.* New York: John Day.

BURNS, JAMES MACGREGOR
1978   *Leadership.* New York: Harper & Row.

CHASE, GORDON
1979   "Implementing a Human Services Program: How Hard Will It Be?" *Public Policy* 27:285–346.

CHASE, GORDON (ADAPTED BY MARY V. KURKJIAN)
1980   "Bromides for Public Managers." Manuscript. John F.

Kennedy School of Government, Harvard University,
August.

CHASE, GORDON, AND ELIZABETH C. REVEAL
1983   *How to Manage in the Public Sector.* New York: Random
House.

CLAPP, GORDON R.
1956   "The Social Scientist and the Administrative Art." In *The
State of the Social Sciences,* ed. Leonard D. White. Chicago: University of Chicago Press.

COHEN, MICHAEL D., JAMES G. MARCH, AND JOHAN P. OLSEN
1972   "A Garbage Can Model of Organizational Choice." In
March (1988, 294–334).

COHEN, STEVEN
1988   *The Effective Public Manager: Achieving Success in Government.* San Francisco: Jossey-Bass.

CORSON, JOHN J.
1952   *Executives for the Federal Service.* New York: Columbia
University Press.

COULAM, ROBERT F.
1977   *Illusions of Choice: The F-111 and the Problem of Weap-
ons Acquisition Reform.* Princeton: Princeton University
Press.

DAHL, ROBERT A.
1947   "The Science of Administration: Three Problems." *Public
Administration Review* 7:1–11.

DAVID, PAUL T., AND ROSS POLLOCK
1957   *Executives for Government.* Washington, D.C.: Brookings
Institution.

DENHARDT, ROBERT B.
1993   *The Pursuit of Significance: Strategies for Managerial Success in Public Organizations.* Belmont, Calif.: Wads-
worth.

DIIULIO, JOHN J., JR.
1987   *Governing Prisons: A Comparative Study of Correctional
Management.* New York: Free Press.

1990   "Leadership and Social Science." *Journal of Policy Analysis and Management* 9:1:116–26.
1994   "Principled Agents: The Cultural Bases of Behavior in a Federal Government Bureaucracy." *Journal of Public Administration Research and Theory* 4:3:277–318.

DiIULIO, JOHN J., JR., DONALD F. KETTL, AND RICHARD P. NATHAN

1994a   *Making Health Reform Work: Implementation Management and Federalism.* CPM 94-1. Washington, D.C.: Brookings Institution.
1994b   "Administrative Principles." In *Making Health Reform Work: The View from the States,* ed. John J. DiIulio, Donald F. Kettl, and Richard P. Nathan, 12–39. Washington, D.C.: Brookings Institution.

DIMOCK, MARSHALL E.

1936   "The Meaning and Scope of Public Administration." In Gaus et al. (1936).

DOBEL, J. PATRICK

1992   Review of *Impossible Jobs in Public Management. Journal of Policy Analysis and Management* 11:1:144–47.

DOIG, JAMESON W., AND ERWIN C. HARGROVE

1987   *Leadership and Innovation: A Biographical Perspective on Entrepreneurs in Government.* Baltimore: Johns Hopkins University Press.

DONAHUE, JOHN D.

1989   *The Privatization Decision: Public Ends, Private Means.* New York: Basic Books.

DOWNS, ANTHONY

1967   *Inside Bureaucracy.* Boston: Little, Brown.

DOWNS, GEORGE W., AND PATRICK D. LARKEY

1986   *The Search for Government Efficiency: From Hubris to Helplessness.* New York: Random House.

DROR, YEHEZKEL

1983   *Public Policymaking Reexamined.* New Brunswick, N.J.: Transaction.

References

DUNLEAVY, PATRICK

1985   "Bureaucrats, Budgets and the Growth of the State: Re-
constructing an Instrumental Model." *British Journal of
Political Science* 15:299–328.

1991   *Democracy, Bureaucracy, and Public Choice.* Englewood
Cliffs, N.J.: Prentice Hall.

EDELMAN, MURRAY

1964   *The Symbolic Uses of Politics.* Urbana: University of Illinois Press.

1988   *Constructing the Political Spectacle.* Chicago: University
of Chicago Press.

EGGERS, ROWLAND

1975   "The Period of Crisis: 1933 to 1945." In Mosher (1975).

ELMORE, RICHARD F.

1979–80 "Backward Mapping: Implementation Research and Policy
Decisions." *Political Science Quarterly* 94:4:69–83.

1986   "Graduate Education in Public Management: Working the
Seams of Government." *Journal of Policy Analysis and
Management* 6:1:69–83.

1991   "Teaching, Learning, and Education for the Public Service." *Journal of Policy Analysis and Management*
10:2:167–80.

EMMERICH, HERBERT

1971   *Federal Organization and Administrative Management.*
University, Ala.: University of Alabama Press.

FAIRLIN, JOHN A.

1905   *The National Administration of the United States of
America.* New York: Macmillan.

FENN, DAN H., JR.

1979   "Finding Where the Power Lies in Government." *Harvard
Business Review* 57:5:144–53.

FISCHER, FRANK

1993   "Citizen Participation and the Democratization of Policy
Expertise: From Theoretical Inquiry to Practical Cases."
Policy Sciences 26:165–87.

FLEISHMAN, JOEL L.

1990   "A New Framework for Integration: Policy Analysis and Public Management." *American Behavioral Scientist* 33:6:733–54.

FOUNTAIN, JANE E.

1994   "Comment: Disciplining Public Management Research." *Journal of Policy Analysis and Management* 13:2:269–77.

FREDERICKSON, H. GEORGE

1991   "The Reissue of Simon, Smithburg, and Thompson's *Public Administration*." *Journal of Public Administration Research and Theory* 1:75–88.

1994   "American Public Administration: Pushing Things Up to Their First Principles." Manuscript. Prepared for the Fall meeting of the National Academy of Public Administration, Washington, D.C., 24 October.

FRIEDRICH, CARL J.

1940   "Public Policy and the Nature of Administrative Responsibility." In *Public Policy 1940*, 3–24. Cambridge, Mass.: Harvard University Press.

FRIEDSON, ELIOT

1974   "Dominant Professions, Bureaucracy, and Client Services." In *Human Service Organizations: A Book of Readings*, ed. Yeheskel Hasenfeld and Richard A. English. Ann Arbor: University of Michigan Press.

1994   *Professionalism Reborn: Theory, Prophecy, and Policy.* Chicago: University of Chicago Press.

GARSON, G. DAVID, AND E. SAMUEL OVERMAN

1983   *Public Management Research in the United States.* New York: Praeger.

GAUS, JOHN M., LEONARD D. WHITE, AND MARSHALL E. DIMOCK

1936   *The Frontiers of Public Administration.* Chicago: University of Chicago Press. Reprint, New York: Russell and Russell, 1967.

GEORGE, R.E.

1916   "Increased Efficiency as a Result of Increased Governmental Functions." *Annals of the American Academy of Political and Social Science* 64:87. Quoted in Short (1923, 29–30).

GERTH, H.H., AND C. WRIGHT MILLS
1946   *From Max Weber: Essays in Sociology.* New York: Oxford University Press.

GOGGIN, MALCOLM L., ANN O'M. BOWMAN, JAMES P. LESTER, AND LAURENCE J. O'TOOLE, JR.
1990   "Studying the Dynamics of Public Policy Implementation: A Third-Generation Approach." In *Implementation and the Policy Process: Opening Up the Black Box,* ed. D. Palumbo and D. Calista, 181–97. Westport, Conn.: Greenwood Press.

GOLDEN, OLIVIA
1990   "Innovation in Public Sector Human Service Programs: The Implications of Innovation by 'Groping Along.'" *Journal of Policy Analysis and Management* 9:2:219–48.

GOLEMBIEWSKI, ROBERT T., AND MICHAEL WHITE
1978   *Cases in Public Management.* 2d ed. Chicago: Rand McNally.

GOODNOW, FRANK J.
1900   *Politics and Administration.* New York: Macmillan.
1905   *The Principles of Administrative Law of the United States.* New York: Putnam's.

GORTNER, HAROLD
1977   *Administration in the Public Sector.* New York: Wiley.

GRAHAM, COLE BLEASE, JR., AND STEVEN W. HAYS
1986   *Managing the Public Organization.* Washington, D.C.: CQ Press.

GRAHAM, GEORGE A.
1941   *Education for the Public Administration.* Chicago: Public Administration Service.

GRIFFITH, ERNEST S.
1939   *The Impasse of Democracy: A Study of the Modern Government in Action.* New York: Harrison-Hilton Books.

GRUBER, JUDITH
1987   *Controlling Bureaucracies: Dilemmas in Democratic Governance.* Berkeley: University of California Press.

GULICK, LUTHER H.
1928   *The National Institute of Public Administration: A Process Report.* New York: The National Institute of Public Administration.
1937   "Notes on the Theory of Organization," in Gulick and Urwick (1937).

GULICK, LUTHER H., AND LYNDALL URWICK, EDS.
1937   *Papers on the Science of Administration.* New York: Institute of Public Administration.

HAASS, RICHARD N.
1994   *The Power to Persuade: How to Be Effective in Government, the Public Sector, or any Unruly Organization.* New York: Houghton Mifflin.

HAMILTON, ALEXANDER
1937   *The Federalist* Nos. 68, 72. Modern Library ed. New York: Random House.

HAMMOND, THOMAS H., AND GARY J. MILLER
1985   "A Social Choice Perspective on Authority and Expertise in Bureaucracy." *American Journal of Political Science* 29: 1–28.

HANNAWAY, JANE
1987   "Supply Creates Demands: An Organizational Process View of Administrative Expansion." *Journal of Policy Analysis and Management* 7:1:118–34.
1989   *Managers Managing: The Workings of an Administrative System.* New York: Oxford University Press.

HANSMANN, HENRY
1986   "The Role of Nonprofit Enterprise." In Susan Rose-Ackerman (1986a, 57–93).

HARDIN, RUSSELL
1982   *Collective Action.* Baltimore: Johns Hopkins University Press.

HARGROVE, ERWIN
  1975   *The Missing Link: The Study of the Implementation of So-
          cial Policy.* Washington, D.C.: Urban Institute.

HARGROVE, ERWIN C., AND JOHN C. GLIDEWELL
  1990   *Impossible Jobs in Public Management.* Lawrence: Univer-
          sity Press of Kansas.

HECKATHORN, DOUGLAS D., AND STEVEN M. MASER
  1990   "The Contractual Architecture of Public Policy: A Critical
          Reconstruction of Lowi's Typology." *Journal of Politics*
          52:4:1101–23.

HECLO, HUGH
  1977   *A Government of Strangers: Executive Politics in Washing-
          ton.* Washington, D.C.: Brookings Institution.
  1979   "Issue Networks and the Executive Establishment," ed.
          Anthony King. In *The New American Political System,*
          Washington, D.C.: American Enterprise Institute for
          Public Policy Research.
  1985   "An Executive's Success Can Have Costs." In *The Reagan
          Presidency and the Governing of America,* ed. Lester M.
          Salamon and Michael S. Lund, 371–74. Washington,
          D.C.: Urban Institute.

HESS, STEPHEN
  1976   *Organizing the Presidency.* Washington, D.C.: Brookings
          Institution.

HEYMANN, PHILIP B.
  1987   *The Politics of Public Management.* New Haven: Yale
          University Press.

HILL, JOHN PHILIP
  1916   *The Federal Executive.* Boston: Houghton Mifflin.

HOLMSTROM, BENGT, AND PAUL MILGROM
  1991   "Multitask Principal-Agent Analysis: Incentive Contracts,
          Asset Ownership, and Job Design." *Journal of Law,
          Economics, and Organization* 7 (Special Issue): 24–52.

HOLTON, GERALD
  1988   *Thematic Origins of Scientific Thought: Kepler to Ein-
          stein.* Rev. ed. Cambridge, Mass.: Harvard University
          Press.

HORN, MURRAY A., AND KENNETH A. SHEPSLE

1989   "Commentary on 'Administrative Arrangements and the Political Control of Agencies': Administrative Process and Organizational Form as Legislative Responses to Agency Costs." *Virginia Law Review* 75:499–508.

HUDSON, LIAM, AND BERNADINE JACOT

1991   *The Way Men Think: Intellect, Intimacy, and the Erotic Imagination.* New Haven: Yale University Press.

INGRAM, HELEN

1990   "Implementation: A Review and Suggested Framework." In Lynn and Wildavsky (1990, 462–80).

KAUFMAN, HERBERT

1981   *The Administrative Behavior of Federal Bureau Chiefs.* Washington, D.C.: Brookings Institution.

KELMAN, STEVEN

1987   *Making Public Policy: A Hopeful View of American Government.* New York: Basic Books.

1990   *Procurement and Public Management: The Fear of Discretion and the Quality of Government Performance.* Washington, D.C.: AEI Press.

1991   "The Prescriptive Message." A contribution to "The Public Administration of James Q. Wilson: A Symposium on *Bureaucracy.*" *Public Administration Review* 51:3:195–96.

KETTL, DONALD F.

1990   "The Peril—and Prospects—of Public Administration." *Public Administration Review* 50:4:411–19.

KILPATRICK, FRANKLIN P., MILTON C. CUMMINGS, JR., AND M. KENT JENNINGS

1964a   *Source Book of a Study of Occupational Values and the Image of the Federal Service.* Washington, D.C.: Brookings Institution.

1964b   *The Image of the Federal Service.* Washington, D.C.: Brookings Institution.

KLINGNER, DONALD

1983   *Public Administration: A Management Approach.* Boston: Houghton Mifflin.

KNOKE, DAVID
1990   *Political Networks: The Structural Perspective.* New York: Cambridge University Press.

KNOTT, JACK H., AND GARY J. MILLER
1987   *Reforming Bureaucracy: The Politics of Institutional Choice.* Englewood Cliffs, N.J.: Prentice Hall.

LAUMANN, EDWARD O., AND DAVID KNOKE
1987   *The Organizational State: Social Choice in National Policy Domains.* Madison: University of Wisconsin Press.

LANDAU, MARTIN
1973   "On the Concept of the Self-Correcting Organization." *Public Administration Review* 33:533–42.

LAWLOR, EDWARD F.
1994   "The Theory, Implementation, and Evaluation of Health Alliances." Manuscript. Center for Health Administration Studies, University of Chicago.

LAWTON, FREDERICK J.
1954   "The Role of the Administrators in the Federal Government." *Public Administration Review* 14:112–18.

LAX, DAVID A., AND JAMES K. SEBENIUS
1986   *The Manager as Negotiator: Bargaining for Cooperation and Competitive Gain.* New York: Free Press.

LEVIN, MARTIN A.
1986   "Effective Implementation and Its Limits." In *Bureaucratic and Governmental Reform,* ed. Donald J. Calista, 215–41. Greenwich, Conn.: JAI Press.

LEVIN, MARTIN A., AND BARBARA FERMAN
1985   *The Political Hand: Policy Implementation and Youth Employment Programs.* New York: Pergamon Press.
1986   "The Political Hand: Policy Implementation and Youth Employment Programs." *Journal of Policy Analysis and Management* 5:2:311–25.

LEVIN, MARTIN A., AND MARY BRYNA SANGER
1994   *Making Government Work: How Entrepreneurial Executives Turn Bright Ideas into Real Results.* San Francisco: Jossey-Bass.

LEVITT, THEODORE
    1976   "Management and the 'Post-Industrial' Society." *The Public Interest* 44:69–103.

LIGHT, PAUL C.
    1995   *Thickening Government: Federal Hierarchy and the Diffusion of Accountability.* Washington, D.C.: Brookings Institution.

LINDBLOM, CHARLES E.
    1965   *The Intelligence of Democracy: Decision Making through Mutual Adjustment.* New York: Free Press.
    1981   "Comments on Decisions in Organizations." In *Perspectives on Organization Design and Behavior,* ed. Andrew H. Van de Ven and William F. Joyce. New York: Wiley.
    1990   *Inquiry and Change: The Troubled Attempt to Understand and Shape Society.* New Haven: Yale University Press.

LINDER, STEPHEN H., AND B. GUY PETERS
    1989   "Instruments of Government: Perceptions and Contexts." *Journal of Public Policy* 9:1:35–58.

LYNN, LAURENCE E., JR.
    1980   *Designing Public Policy: A Casebook on the Role of Policy Analysis.* Santa Monica, Calif.: Goodyear.
    1982   "Government Executives as Gamesmen: A Metaphor for Analyzing Managerial Behavior." *Journal of Policy Analysis and Management* 1:4:482–95.
    1985   "The Reagan Administration and the Renitent Bureaucracy." In *The Reagan Presidency and the Governing of America,* ed. Lester M. Salamon and Michael S. Lund, 339–70. Washington, D.C.: Urban Institute Press.
    1987a   *Managing Public Policy.* Boston: Little, Brown.
    1987b   "Public Management: What Do We Know? What Should We Know? And How Will We Know It?" *Journal of Policy Analysis and Management* 7:1:178–87.
    1989   "Symposium: The Craft of Public Management." *Journal of Policy Analysis and Management* 8:2:284–306.
    1990   "Managing the Social Safety Net: The Job of the Social Welfare Executive." In Hargrove and Glidewell (1990, 133–51).
    1992   "Strategic Management." Working Paper No. 92-4. Irving

B. Harris Graduate School of Public Policy Studies, University of Chicago, 10 May.

1993   "Policy Achievement as a Collective Good: A Strategic Perspective on Managing Social Programs." In *Public Management Theory,* ed. Barry Bozeman. San Francisco: Jossey-Bass.

LYNN, LAURENCE E., JR., AND BARBARA KOREMENOS
1994   "Leadership of a State Agency: An Analysis Using Game Theory." Working Paper No. 94-3. Irving B. Harris Graduate School of Public Policy Studies, University of Chicago.

LYNN, LAURENCE E., JR., AND JOHN M. SEIDL
1977   " 'Bottom-line' Management for Public Agencies." *Harvard Business Review* 55:1:144–53.

LYNN, LAURENCE E., JR., AND RICHARD L. SMITH
1982   "Can the Secretary of Defense Make a Difference?" *International Security* 7:1:45–69.

LYNN, NAOMI B., AND AARON WILDAVSKY
1990   *Public Administration: The State of the Discipline.* Chatham, N.J.: Chatham House.

MACMAHON, ARTHUR W., AND JOHN D. MILLETT
1939   *Federal Administrators: A Biographical Approach to the Problem of Departmental Management.* New York: Columbia University Press.

MAJONE, GIANDOMENICO
1980   "Introduction." In *Pitfalls of Analysis,* ed. Giandomenico Majone and Edward S. Quade. New York: Wiley.

MANN, DEAN E. (WITH JAMESON W. DOIG)
1965   *The Assistant Secretaries.* Washington, D.C.: Brookings Institution.

MANSFIELD, HARVEY C., JR.
1989   *Taming the Prince: The Ambivalence of Modern Executive Power.* New York: Free Press.

MARCH, JAMES G.
1988   *Decision and Organization.* Oxford, England: Basil Blackwell.

MARCH, JAMES G., AND JOHAN P. OLSEN
  1989   *Rediscovering Institutions.* New York: Free Press.

MARX, FRITZ MORSTEIN, ED.
  1940   *Public Management in the New Democracy.* New York:
          Harper & Brothers.

MAYER, FREDERICK W.
  1992   "Basketball and Public Management: Testing What's Im-
          portant." *Journal of Policy Analysis and Management*
          11:2:322–26.

McCUBBINS, MATHEW D., ROGER G. NOLL, AND BARRY R.
WEINGAST
  1987   "Administrative Procedures as Instruments of Political
          Control." *Journal of Law, Economics, and Organiza-
          tion* 3:2:243–86.
  1989   "Structure and Process, Politics and Policy: Administrative
          Arrangements and the Political Control of Agencies."
          Virginia Law Review 75:431–83.

MECHANIC, DAVID
  1962   "Sources of Power of Lower Participants in Complex Or-
          ganizations." *Administrative Science Quarterly*
          7:4:340–84.

MEIER, KENNETH J.
  1986   *Politics and the Bureaucracy: Policymaking in the Fourth
          Branch of Government.* 2d ed. Monterey, Calif.:
          Brooks/Cole.
  1989   "Bureaucratic Leadership in Public Organizations." In
          *Leadership and Politics: New Perspectives in Political
          Science,* ed. Bryan D. Jones. Lawrence: University Press
          of Kansas.
  1993   "Public Administration Theory and Applied Economics:
          Some Intemperate Remarks." *Administration and Poli-
          tics* 3:1:4–6.

MERIAM, LEWIS
  1938   *Public Personnel Problems: From the Standpoint of the
          Operating Officer.* Washington, D.C.: Brookings Institu-
          tion.

MILLER, GARY

1990   "Administrative Dilemmas: The Role of Political Leadership." In *The Limits of Rationality,* ed. Margaret Levi and Karen Cook. Chicago: University of Chicago Press.

1992   *Managerial Dilemmas: The Political Economy of Hierarchies.* New York: Cambridge University Press.

MILLS, C. WRIGHT

1956   *The Power Elite.* New York: Oxford University Press.

MITNICK, BARRY M., AND ROBERT W. BACKOFF

1984   "The Incentive Relation in Implementation." In *Public Policy Implementation,* ed. George C. Edwards III. Greenwich, Conn.: JAI Press.

MOE, TERRY M.

1990   "The Politics of Structural Choice: Toward a Theory of Public Bureaucracy." In *Organizational Theory: From Chester Barnard to the Present and Beyond,* ed. Oliver W. Williamson, 116–53. New York: Oxford University Press.

1991   "Politics and the Theory of Organization." *Journal of Law, Economics, and Organization* 7:106–29.

1994   "Integrating Politics and Organizations: Positive Theory and Public Administration." *Journal of Public Administration Research and Theory* 4:1:17–25.

MOORE, MARK H.

1984   "A Conception of Public Management." In *Teaching Public Management* (1984, 1–12).

MOSHER, FREDERICK C.

1968   *Democracy and the Public Service.* New York: Oxford University Press.

MOSHER, FREDERICK C., ED.

1975   *American Public Administration: Past, Present, Future.* University, Ala.: University of Alabama Press.

MUNDEL, MARVIN E.

1975   *Measuring and Enhancing the Productivity of Service and Government Organizations.* Tokyo: Asian Productivity Organization.

MURPHY, THOMAS P., DONALD E. NEUCHTERLEIN, AND RONALD J. STUPAK

1978   *Inside the Bureaucracy: The View from the Assistant Secretary's Desk.* Boulder, Colo.: Westview Press.

NATHAN, RICHARD P.

1993   *Turning Promises into Performance: The Management Challenge of Implementing Workfare.* New York: Columbia University Press.

NEUSTADT, RICHARD E.

1978   *Presidential Power.* 2d ed. New York: Wiley.

NOLL, ROGER, AND BARRY WEINGAST

1987   "Rational Actor Theory, Social Norms, and Policy Implementation: Applications to Administrative Processes and Bureaucratic Culture." In *The Economic Approach to Politics: A Critical Reassessment of the Theory of Rational Action,* ed. K.R. Monroe, 237–58. New York: HarperCollins.

NORTH, DOUGLASS C.

1990   "A Transaction Cost Theory of Politics." *Journal of Theoretical Politics* 2:4:355–67.

1991   "Institutions." *Journal of Economic Perspectives* 5:1:97–112.

OLSON, MANCUR

1971   *The Logic of Collective Action.* Cambridge: Harvard University Press.

OSBORNE, DAVID, AND TED GAEBLER

1992   *Reinventing Government: How the Entrepreneurial Spirit Is Transforming the Public Sector.* Reading, Mass.: Addison-Wesley.

OSTROM, ELINOR

1986   "An Agenda for the Study of Institutions." *Public Choice* 48:3–25.

OSTROM, ELINOR, LARRY SCHROEDER, AND SUSAN WYNNE

1993   "Analyzing the Performance of Alternative Institutional Arrangements for Sustaining Rural Infrastructure in Developing Countries." *Journal of Public Administration Research and Theory* 3:1:11–45.

O'TOOLE, LAURENCE J., JR.

1991   "Multiorganizational Policy Implementation: Some Limitations and Possibilities for Rational Choice Contributions." Prepared for the Workshop on Games in Hierarchies and Networks, Max Planck Institut für Gesellschaftsforschung, Köln, Germany, 5–7 September.

1993   "Rational Choice and the Public Management of Interorganizational Networks." Paper prepared for presentation at the National Public Management Research Conference, University of Wisconsin–Madison, 30 September–2 October.

OTT, J. STEVEN, ALBERT C. HYDE, AND JAY M. SHAFRITZ, EDS.

1991   *Public Management: The Essential Readings.* Chicago: Nelson-Hall.

OUCHI, WILLIAM G.

1979   "A Conceptual Framework for the Design of Organizational Control Mechanisms." *Management Science* 25:833–48.

1980   "Markets, Bureaucracies, and Clans." *Administrative Science Quarterly* 25:129–41.

OVERMAN, E. SAM

1984   "Public Management: What's New and Different?" *Public Administration Review* 44:3:275–78.

OVERMAN, E. SAM, AND KATHY J. BOYD

1994   "Best Practice Research and Postbureaucratic Reform." *Journal of Public Administration Research and Theory* 4:1:67–83.

PERRY, JAMES L., AND KENNETH L. KRAEMER

1983   *Public Management: Public and Private Perspectives.* Palo Alto, Calif.: Mayfield.

PETERS, THOMAS J., AND ROBERT H. WATERMAN, JR.

1982   *In Search of Excellence: Lessons from America's Best-Run Companies.* New York: Harper & Row.

POWELL, WALTER W.

1990   "Neither Market nor Hierarchy: Network Forms of Organization." In *Research in Organizational Behavior* 12, ed. B. Staw and L.L. Cummings, 295–326.

POWELL, WALTER W., AND PAUL J. DiMAGGIO, EDS.
1991   *The New Institutionalism in Organizational Analysis.*
        Chicago: University of Chicago Press.

PRESSMAN, JEFFREY L., AND AARON WILDAVSKY
1973   *Implementation.* Berkeley: University of California Press.

PRICE, DON K.
1975   "1984 and Beyond: Social Engineering or Political
        Values?" In Mosher, ed. (1975, 223–52).

RAINEY, HAL G.
1989   "Public Management: Recent Research on the Political
        Context and Managerial Roles, Structures, and Be-
        haviors." *Journal of Management* 15:2:229–50.
1990   "Public Management: Recent Developments and Current
        Prospects." In Lynn and Wildavsky, eds. (1990,
        157–84).
1991   *Understanding and Managing Public Organizations.* San
        Francisco: Jossey-Bass.
1992   Review of *Refounding Public Administration, Governing
        Public Organizations: Politics, Structures, and Institu-
        tional Design,* and *Public Administration: Challenges,
        Choices, Consequences. Journal of Policy Analysis and
        Management* 11:1:147–53.

REHFUSS, JOHN
1989   *The Job of the Public Manager.* Chicago: Dorsey Press.

REICH, ROBERT B.
1990   *Public Management in a Democratic Society.* Englewood
        Cliffs, N.J.: Prentice Hall.

REICH, ROBERT B., ED.
1988   *The Power of Public Ideas.* Cambridge, Mass.: Ballinger.

RICHARDSON, ELLIOT L.
1976   *The Creative Balance.* New York: Holt, Rinehart and
        Winston.

RIGGS, FRED W.
1994   "Why Has Bureaucracy Not Smothered Democracy in the
        United States?" In *Comparative Public Administration:
        Putting U.S. Public Policy and the Implementation in
        Context,* ed. Randall Baker. Westport, Conn.: Praeger.

References

RIKER, WILLIAM H.
  1986   *The Art of Political Manipulation*. New Haven: Yale University Press.

ROBERTS, ALASDAIR
  1995   " 'Civic Discovery' as a Rhetorical Strategy." *Journal of Policy Analysis and Management* 14:2:291–307.

ROHR, JOHN A.
  1986   *To Run a Constitution*. Lawrence: University Press of Kansas.

ROSE-ACKERMAN, SUSAN
  1986a *The Economics of Nonprofit Institutions: Studies in Structure and Policy*. New York: Oxford University Press.
  1986b "Reforming Public Bureaucracy through Economic Incentives?" *Journal of Law, Economics, and Organization* 2:1:131–61.

ROSENBLOOM, DAVID H.
  1993   "Have an Administrative Rx? Don't Forget the Politics." *Public Administration Review* 43:6:507.
  1994   "The Evolution of the Administrative State and Transformations of Administrative Law." In *Handbook of Regulation and Administrative Law*, ed. David H. Rosenbloom and Richard D. Schwartz, 3–36. New York: Marcel Dekker.

ROSENTHAL, STEPHEN R.
  1982   *Managing Government Operations*. Glenview, Ill.: Scott, Foresman.

ROURKE, FRANCIS E.
  1984   *Bureaucracy, Politics, and Public Policy*. Boston: Little, Brown.

RUMSFELD, DONALD H.
  1976   "Rumsfeld's Rules: Rules (and Observations of Donald Rumsfeld [and Others])." Manuscript, n.p.

SABATIER, PAUL A., AND DANIEL A. MAZMANIAN
  1980   "The Implementation of Public Policy: A Framework of Analysis." *Policy Studies Journal* 8:4:538–60.

SALAMON, LESTER M.
  1981   "Rethinking Public Management: Third-Party Government

and the Changing Forms of Government Action." *Public Policy* 29:3:255–75.

SALANCIK, G.R., AND J. PFEFFER
1977   "Constraints on Administrative Discretion: The Limited Influence of Mayors on City Budgets." *Urban Affairs Quarterly* 12:475–98.

SAPOLSKY, HARVEY M.
1967   "Organizational Structure and Innovation." *Journal of Business* 40:4:497–510.

SAWHILL, ISABEL V.
1989   "Strengthening the Three-Legged Stool of Policy Analysis, Organization, and Leadership." *Journal of Policy Analysis and Management* 8:3:501–4.

SCHELLING, THOMAS C.
1960   *The Strategy of Conflict.* Cambridge: Harvard University Press.

SCHICK, ALLEN
1971   *Budget Innovation in the States.* Washington, D.C.: Brookings Institution.

SCHNEIDER, ANNE, AND HELEN INGRAM
1990   "Behavioral Assumptions of Policy Tools." *Journal of Politics* 52:2:10–29.

SCHOENBERG, SANDRA P.
1973   "A Typology of Leadership Style in Public Organizations." In *Organization and Managerial Innovation,* ed. L.A. Rowe and W.B. Boise, 177–86. Santa Monica, Calif.: Goodyear.

SCHON, DONALD A.
1983   *The Reflective Practitioner: How Professionals Think in Action.* New York: Basic Books.

SCHON, DONALD, AND MARTIN REIN
1994   *Frame Reflection: Toward the Resolution of Intractable Policy Controversies.* New York: Basic Books.

SCHUMM, L. PHILIP
1990   "Applied Network Analysis." School of Business, University of Chicago.

SCOTT, W. RICHARD

    1992   *Organizations: Rational, Natural, and Open Systems.* 3d
               ed. Englewood Cliffs, N.J.: Prentice Hall.

SECKLER-HUDSON, CATHERYN

    1955   *Organization and Management: Theory and Practice.*
               Washington, D.C.: American University Press. Reprinted
               in *Classics of Public Administration,* ed. J.M. Shafritz
               and Albert C. Hyde, 203–11. Pacific Grove, Calif.:
               Brooks/Cole, 1992.

SELZNICK, PHILIP

    1984   *Leadership in Administration: A Sociological Interpreta-
               tion.* Berkeley: University of California Press.

SHERWOOD, FRANK P.

    1990   "The Half-Century's 'Great Books' in Public Administra-
               tion." *Public Administration Review* 50:2:249–64.

SHORT, LLOYD MILTON

    1923   *The Development of National Administration Organiza-
               tion in the United States.* Baltimore: Johns Hopkins
               University Press.

SIMON, HERBERT A.

    1946   "The Proverbs of Administration." *Public Administration
               Review* 6:53–67.

    1964   "On the Concept of Organizational Goal." *Administrative
               Science Quarterly* 9:1–11.

    1976   *Administrative Behavior: A Study of Decision-Making
               Processes in Administrative Organization.* 3d ed. New
               York: Free Press.

SIMON, HERBERT A., DONALD W. SMITHBURG, AND VICTOR A.
THOMPSON

    1950   *Public Administration.* New York: Knopf.

SIMON, HERBERT A., VICTOR A. THOMPSON, AND DONALD W.
SMITHBURG

    1991   *Public Administration.* New Brunswick, N.J.: Transaction.

SKOWRONEK, STEPHEN

    1982   *Building a New American State: The Expansion of Ad-
               ministrative Capacities, 1877–1920.* New York: Cam-
               bridge University Press.

STANLEY, DAVID T.
1964   *The Higher Civil Service.* Washington, D.C.: Brookings Institution.

STANLEY, DAVID T., DEAN E. MANN, AND JAMESON W. DOIG
1967   *Men Who Govern.* Washington, D.C.: Brookings Institution.

STARLING, J. D.
1982   *Managing the Public Sector.* 2d ed. Homewood, Ill.: Dorsey Press.

STEIN, HAROLD, ED.
1952   *Public Administration and Policy Development: A Case Book.* New York: Harcourt, Brace.

STEINBRUNER, JOHN D.
1974   *The Cybernetic Theory of Decision: New Dimensions of Political Analysis.* Princeton: Princeton University Press.

STINCHCOMBE, ARTHUR L.
1986   "Social Structure and the Founding of Organizations." In *Stratification and Organizations,* ed. Arthur L. Stinchcombe, 196–230. New York: Cambridge University Press.

STOKES, DONALD E.
1986   "Political and Organizational Analysis in the Policy Curriculum." *Journal of Policy Analysis and Management* 6:1:45–55.

STOKEY, EDITH, AND RICHARD ZECKHAUSER
1978   *A Primer for Policy Analysis.* New York: Norton.

STONE, ALICE B., AND DONALD C. STONE
1975   "Early Development of Education in Public Administration." In Mosher (1975).

STRAUSSMAN, JEFFREY D.
1993   " 'Management by Groping Along': The Limits of a Metaphor." *Governance* 6:2:154–71.

TAYLOR, FREDERICK W.
1911   *The Principles of Scientific Management.* New York: Harper & Brothers.

References

Teaching Public Management
1984 Proceedings of a Workshop to Assess Materials and Strategies for Teaching Public Management, Seattle, 9–11 May. Public Policy and Management Program for Case and Course Development, Boston University, 1–12.

Tocqueville, Alexis de
1969 *Democracy in America.* New York: Harper & Row.

U.S. Commission on Organization of the Executive Branch of the Government
1949 *General Management of the Executive Branch.* Washington, D.C.: Government Printing Office.
1955 *Task Force Report on Personnel and Civil Service.* Washington: D.C.: Government Printing Office.

Vickers, Sir Geoffrey
1983 *The Art of Judgment: A Study of Policy Making.* London: Harper & Row.

Wallace, Schuyler, C.
1941 *Federal Departmentalization.* New York: Columbia University Press.

Wamsley, Gary L.
1990 "The Agency Perspective: Public Administrators as Agential Leaders." In *Refounding Public Administration,* ed. Gary L. Wamsley et al. Newbury Park, Calif.: Sage.

Warner, W. Lloyd, Paul P. Van Riper, Norman H. Martin, and Orvis F. Collins
1963 *The American Federal Executive.* New Haven: Yale University Press.

Weimer, David L.
1992a "Claiming Races, Broiler Contracts, Heresthetics, and Habits: Ten Concepts for Policy Design." *Policy Sciences* 25:135–59.
1992b "Political Science, Practitioner Skill, and Public Management." *Public Administration Review* 52:3:240–45.

Weimer, David L., and Aidan R. Vining
1989 *Policy Analysis: Concepts and Practice.* Englewood Cliffs, N.J.: Prentice Hall.

WEINBERG, MARTHA WAGNER

1977 *Managing the State.* Cambridge: MIT Press.

1983 "Public Management and Private Management: A Diminishing Gap?" *Journal of Policy Analysis and Management* 3:1:107–15.

WEISS, JANET A.

1981 "Substance vs. Symbol in Administrative Reform." *Policy Sciences* 7:21–45.

1982 "Coping with Complexity: An Experimental Study of Public Policy Decision Making." *Journal of Policy Analysis and Management* 2:1:66–87.

1987 "Pathways to Cooperation among Public Agencies." *Journal of Policy Analysis and Management* 7:1:94–117.

1989 "The Powers of Problem Definition: The Case of Government Paperwork." *Policy Sciences* 22: 97–121.

1990 "Ideas and Inducements in Mental Health Policy." *Journal of Policy Analysis and Management* 9:2:178–200.

WEISS, JANET A., AND JUDITH E. GRUBER

1984 "Using Knowledge for Control in Fragmented Policy Arenas." *Journal of Policy Analysis and Management* 3:2:225–47.

WHITE, LEONARD D.

1936 "The Meaning of Principles in Public Administration." In Gaus et al. (1936).

1948 *The Federalists.* New York: Macmillan.

1950 *Introduction to the Study of Public Administration.* 3d ed. New York: Macmillan.

1954 *The Jacksonians.* New York: Macmillan.

1958 *The Republican Era, 1869–1901.* New York: Macmillan.

WILDAVSKY, AARON

1964 *The Politics of the Budgetary Process.* Boston: Little, Brown.

1985 "The Once and Future School of Public Policy." *The Public Interest* 79:25–41.

WILKINS, ALAN L., AND WILLIAM G. OUCHI

1983 "Efficient Cultures: Exploring the Relationship between

Culture and Organizational Performance." *Administrative Science Quarterly* 28:468–81.

WILSON, JAMES Q.

1989   *Bureaucracy: What Government Agencies Do and Why They Do It.* New York: Basic Books.

WILSON, WOODROW

1887   "The Study of Administration." *Political Science Quarterly* 2:1:197–222.

YATES, DOUGLAS, JR.

1982   *Bureaucratic Democracy: The Search for Democracy and Efficiency in American Government.* Cambridge: Harvard University Press.

1987   *The Politics of Management.* San Francisco: Jossey-Bass.

Index

Index

Hamilton, Alexander, 9, 11, 12, 20, 25, 89
Hammond, Thomas H., 100, 107, 116
Hannaway, Jane, 77
Hansmann, Henry, 120
Harding, Warren G., 16
Hargrove, Erwin C., 47, 70, 92
Hays, Steven W., 42
Health-care policy, 137–38
Heckathorn, Douglas D., 118
Heclo, Hugh, 33, 36–37, 71, 91, 128
Hess, Stephen, 18
Heuristics, application of, 100–101
Heymann, Philip B., 72
Hobbes, Thomas, 25
Holmstrom, Bengt, 116–17
Holton, Gerald, 107
Hoover, Herbert, 34–35
Hoover, J. Edgar, 145
Hoover Commission, 19, 34–35
Horn, Murray A., 121–22
Hyde, Albert C., 39–40, 87

Illinois Department on Aging, 139–41
Ingram, Helen, 48, 51
Institute for Government Research, 29
Institutions
  conceptualization of, 124
  forms of, 120
  see also Organizations
Issue networks, 33, 128

JOBS program, 134, 135–36
Jordan, Vernon, 85
Jurisdiction
  defined, 144
  issues of, 159
  knowledge base for, 144–49
  tensions within, 157–58

Kagan, Robert A., 74–75, 79, 135–36
Kaufman, Herbert, 129
Keep, Charles Hallam, 15
Keep Commission, 15
Kelman, Steven, 59, 78–80, 96, 136, 149

Kettl, Donald F., 87, 137
Knoke, David, 33, 126
Knott, Jack H., 46
Koppel, Ted, 85
Koremenos, Barbara, 139–41
Kraemer, Kenneth L., 38, 39

Laumann, Edward O., 33
Lawlor, Edward, 137–38
Lax, David A., 136
Leadership, vs. organization, 69–80
Learning, approaches to, 112–13
Legislative Reorganization Act of 1946, 17
Levin, Martin A., 69–70, 84, 90, 94, 107, 157–58
Light, Paul C., 22
Lindblom, Charles E., 90, 92–93, 128, 163–64
Linder, Stephen H., 52
Long, Norton E., 31
Lynn, Laurence E., Jr., 67, 128, 139–41

McCubbins, Mathew D., 121–22
Madison, James, 25
Majone, Giandomenico, 93
March, James G., 124, 128–29
Marx, Fritz Morstein, 31, 38
Maser, Steven M., 118
Mayer, Frederick W., 102
Mazmanian, Daniel A., 47–48
Mechanic, David, 122
Meier, Kenneth J., 45–46, 153–54
Mental discipline, exercise of, 110–11
Milgrom, Paul, 116–17
Miller, Gary J., 46, 115, 117, 123
Mills, C. Wright, 32
Mitnick, Barry M., 49
Moore, Mark H., 57–59, 64, 88, 95
Moses, Robert, 145

Nathan, Richard P., 86, 107, 134–35, 137
National Performance Review, 19
National Public Management Research Conferences, 4

Index

About the Author

Laurence E. Lynn, Jr., has been Professor of Social Service Administration and of Public Policy Studies at the University of Chicago since 1983. He served as Dean of the School of Social Service Administration from 1983 to 1988. Formerly, he was Professor of Public Policy and Chairman of the Public Policy Program at Harvard University's John F. Kennedy School of Government.

Lynn has held senior positions within the federal government, including Deputy Assistant Secretary of Defense (Economics and Resource Analysis); Director of Program Analysis at the National Security Council; Assistant Secretary (Planning and Evaluation), Department of Health, Education and Welfare; and Assistant Secretary (Program Development and Budget), Department of the Interior. He has been a consultant to federal, state, and local agencies, has organized and served on the faculties of executive and management development institutes and seminars, has chaired National Academy of Sciences/National Research Council committees on Child Development Research and Public Policy and on National Urban Policy, and has participated in the activities of many community organizations.

Professor Lynn is the author of *The State and Human Services; Designing Public Policy; Managing the Public's Business;* and *Managing Public Policy.* He is coauthor of *The President as Policy Maker* and editor or co-editor of *Knowledge and Policy: The Uncertain Connection, Urban Change and Poverty,* and *Inner-City Poverty in the United States.* He has published numerous articles on his primary research interests: public policy analysis and planning, the strategic management of public bureaucracies, leadership and learning styles, and social welfare policy and administration.

Lynn is a graduate of the University of California at Berkeley and holds a Ph.D. in Economics from Yale University. He is past president of the Association for Public Policy Analysis and Management and a winner of its Vernon Prize. He is also a fellow of the National Academy of Public Administration. He has received the Secretary of Defense Meritorious Civilian Service Award and a Presidential Certificate of Distinguished Achievement.